Stock Market Investing For Complete Beginners

Savannaha .U Thompsonu

Introduction

Welcome to this book, a comprehensive guide that will empower you to navigate the exciting world of stock market investing with confidence and knowledge. In this book, we will demystify the complexities of the stock market, equip you with essential tools and strategies, and guide you towards making informed investment decisions.

Understanding why you should invest in stocks is the first step on your journey. We will explore the compelling reasons why stocks can be a powerful wealth-building tool, offering the potential for long-term growth and financial independence. By recognizing the benefits of stock market investing, you can unlock a world of opportunities.

Before diving into the world of stocks, it's crucial to understand what stocks are and how they function. We will provide a comprehensive overview, explaining the concepts of shares, ownership, dividends, and market dynamics. By grasping the fundamentals, you will gain a solid foundation for successful investing.

Knowing yourself is essential when it comes to investing. We will guide you through a process of self-assessment, helping you identify your risk tolerance, investment goals, and time horizon. Understanding your unique financial profile will enable you to make investment decisions aligned with your individual needs and preferences.

Stocks come in various categories, each with its own characteristics and considerations. We will categorize stocks and explore different types, such as blue-chip stocks, growth stocks, and income stocks. By understanding the distinctions, you can make informed choices that align with your investment objectives.

Analyzing and trading stocks require a strategic approach and a clear understanding of risk management. We will delve into techniques for analyzing stocks, including fundamental and technical analysis. Additionally, we will explore how to allocate risk capital effectively, ensuring you protect your investments while maximizing potential returns.

Introducing the Stock Investing Tiers, we will guide you through a structured approach to stock picking. From buying the market through index funds in Tier 1 to building your own stock picker/trader algo in Tier 7, we will explore each level's strategies, risks, and potential rewards. By understanding the tiers, you can choose an approach that suits your investment style and goals.

Protecting your investment is crucial in stock market investing. We will discuss the importance of diversification, portfolio management, and position sizing. These risk management techniques will help safeguard your capital and minimize potential losses. By implementing these strategies, you can navigate market volatility with confidence.

Regularly reviewing your investment portfolio is essential for maintaining a healthy and successful investment journey. We will explore the importance of ongoing monitoring, evaluating performance, and making adjustments when necessary. By staying proactive and adaptive, you can optimize your investment strategy for long-term success.

Case studies will provide real-world examples of stock market investing. We will analyze successful and cautionary tales to extract valuable lessons and insights. By studying these cases, you can gain a deeper understanding of market dynamics and make more informed decisions.

Avoiding common mistakes is crucial for your investment success. We will discuss common pitfalls and share practical tips to help you steer clear of costly errors. By learning from the mistakes of others, you can minimize risks and maximize your chances of achieving your financial goals.

The rise of millennials and recent phenomena like the GameStop saga have had a significant impact on the stock market. We will explore these trends and their implications for investors. By understanding the evolving landscape, you can position yourself to leverage emerging opportunities.

As you progress on your investing journey, it's important to take the next steps and continuously refine your approach. We will provide guidance on ongoing education, staying informed, and adapting to market changes. By embracing a growth mindset and continuously learning, you can unlock your full potential as an investor.

This book is your comprehensive guide to navigating the stock market with confidence. By understanding the fundamentals, adopting effective strategies, and protecting your investments, you can build a strong foundation for long-term financial success. Get ready to embark on an exciting journey towards wealth creation and achieving your financial dreams.

Contents

CHAPTER 1–WHY SHOULD YOU INVEST IN STOCKS?

Bill Gates. Warren Buffett. Jeff Bezos. Mark Zuckerberg. Carlos Helu-4 of the world's richest men. How did they get there? Their roads to wealth are all different, but they do have one thing in common. They all own stock in companies-possibly ones they created, or ones they just bought into-but they are all owners.

Ownership is what made them rich.

Now, you and I may not be blessed enough to create the next Amazon or Microsoft, but by investing in companies like these, we can benefit by being owners. Owning stock in a company is a great way to achieve long term wealth.

Just how good is it? Take a look at the chart below. A $10,000 bank deposit in 2009, grew to $11,123 in 2019. But if you put the same $10,000 in the US stock market, you'd now find yourself with $40,967.

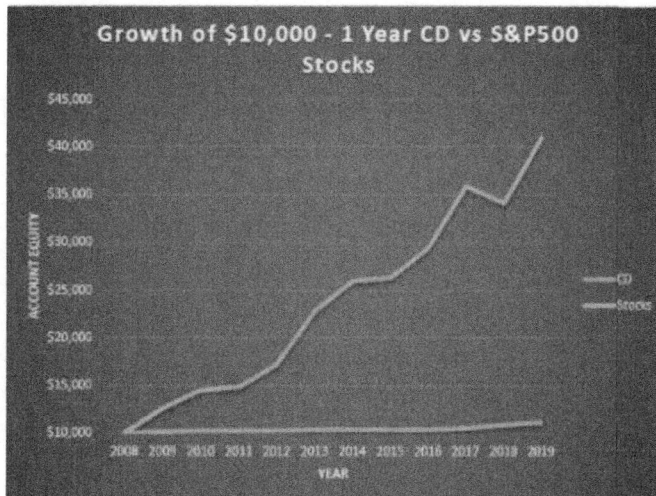

Figure 1- Growth of Bank CD vs. S&P500

Over the long term, owning stocks protects you from the ravages of inflation, and grows at a substantial rate. Let's examine each one of these advantages in detail.

Overcome The Effects Of Inflation

Back in 1970, a gallon of gas in the US cost around 35 cents per gallon. You could fill up your tank for around $5 or $6. In 2019, that same tank costs $40-$50.

Food, clothes and practically every item you buy suffers from the same curse as gasoline-inflation. Over time, items become more expensive. For each of the last 8 decades, prices have risen in the US by 2% to 7% on an annual basis. Some expenses, such as healthcare and college tuition, are skyrocketing at even higher rates.

So, a dollar you earn today will be worth much less 10 or 20 years in the future. Put your money in the bank, earning 1-2% per year, and you will be extremely lucky to just breakeven, when you consider its purchasing power. You need to (and can do) better!

Capital Appreciation-Grow Your Money

Owning stocks can be the solution to growing your money. Instead of 1-2% per year, over time stocks have returned 10% per year. While no one can predict the future, chances are stocks will continue to grow at a similar rate. As the US economy grows, and technology fuels innovation (and vice versa), having ownership in companies will continue to be a good bet.

Not All Roses

Put your money in the bank, and disregarding the effects of inflation or a total currency collapse, you'll never lose money. It might be a slow grind upwards, but with cash in the bank you'll never fall backwards.

In contrast, stock prices don't always increase. Sometimes they go down, and sometimes those moves are quick, violent and large.

You could easily get stuck in a "drawdown"-a period where your account is worth less than you had at its peak. Not so with a bank account.

Companies can go bankrupt and your ownership stake can become worthless. So, even with all its advantages, stock ownership is not without its risks.

Case in point: let's say you invested in the stock market in late 2007, right at the peak before the Financial Crisis. A "buy and hold" investor would need 5.5 years to get back to even.   And, at one point you would have been down a whopping 57%! Would you emotionally survive a drawdown that large and that long? Certainly, stock ownership is not for the faint of heart.

More Than Just Money

Some argue stock ownership is a patriotic endeavor.   Investing in your country and helping its companies grow is a great thing to do. It helps both the country and future generations. It is something nice to be sure, but probably not your primary reason to own stock.

Your primary reason to own stock is to possess more money at the end than what you started with. Plain and simple.

So, let's see how this stock market works, and how you can get started.

CHAPTER 2-WHAT EXACTLY ARE STOCKS?

It starts with an individual or small group of people. Maybe it originates in a garage, like Hewlett Packard or Amazon did. Over 600,000 new ones are created each year. I'm talking about businesses. From single person pursuits to large corporations, new businesses are constantly popping up, fueling the economy's growth.

Each business is owned by someone, or more likely, multiple people. The ownership structure is set up in the articles of incorporation for the business. This is typically set up as shares of stock. A single person may own the whole company, or 100% of the stock. Or, multiple people (or companies) own the stock, each with a percentage ownership stake.

As the business grows, owners might sell their stock, transfer it to others, etc. Or, they may decide to offer it to the public. In an Initial Public Offering (IPO), a certain percentage of stock is made available to the public. This stock is bought and sold on a stock exchange. There are three major exchanges in the United States: the New York Stock Exchange (NYSE), the Nasdaq stock exchange (NASDAQ) and the American Stock Exchange (AMEX).

So, while Hewlett Packard started in a garage as a private company, it eventually grew and became a publicly traded company. Today, you can buy a piece of Hewlett Packard on the NYSE (ticker HPQ). I'll later describe this process.

As an owner of stock in a company, you obtain rights and responsibilities. These depend on the type of stock and the amount of stock you own. For most retail traders, the rights include receiving any dividends the company pays out, and the right to vote on certain aspects of the corporation (such as selecting the company's Board of Directors). Some companies even offer special perks to stockholders, such as discounts.

Stock ownership can easily get confusing. Some companies offer different classes of stock. For example, some companies list preferred stock. Others just offer common stock. Still more provide different classes of stock with different voting rights. All of these have unique features, advantages and disadvantages.

The nice thing is that these different classes, if available, are given unique stock symbols at the exchange. This standardization allows easy transfer of stock. Every share of McDonald's (MCD) stock is the same. Therefore, you don't necessarily need to know all the details of your stock, although there definitely can be advantages in owning one class of stock versus another class.

But just because you own stock in McDonald's, it does not mean you are able to go into a store and start bossing workers around. Stockholders are not involved with day-to-day operations or management of the company. You are an investor, not an active participant. With your stock purchase, you provided capital (money) to the company to fund its operations. But that is where your responsibility ends. The CEO will never call you and ask you to pay some bills, and you won't be required to start flipping hamburgers when a worker calls in sick!

The nice thing is that the company gets to use your money, and in return, if the value of the company goes up, you can sell your ownership stake at a profit. But what about cases where the stock price goes down, or the company goes bankrupt? In those cases, you will lose some or all of your investment. But, you can never lose more than your initial investment. That is a nice feature-no debt collector will come after you just because you own stock in a bankrupt company.

Buying and Selling Publicly Traded Stock

To sum up, owning stock is basically owning a tiny piece of a corporation. If you want to buy or sell publicly traded stock, you do it thru a stock exchange, with a broker's help. This process scares many people. I was petrified the first time I opened a stock trading account. The truth is that nowadays it is really simple and easy to open a stock trading account.

Just follow the simple steps below to open a stock account and place trades in a stock.

Start With Funds

Obviously, you need money to invest in stocks. I'll discuss a proven approach to obtaining risk capital in the next chapters, but there is little point trying to invest without RISK capital. Note the capitalization-RISK. This is money you can afford to lose. You are not happy if you lose it, but it should not impact your day-to-day life. Using next month's rent money to buy stocks is just gambling, and a dumb idea, even by gambling standards. Open a stock account ONLY with money you do not mind losing.

How much to start with? Many brokerages require a minimum which may be $1,000, $5,000 or more. You must research various brokerages, and the minimums for the various accounts they offer.

One other point to consider is your trading style.   If you are going to be an active day trader, be aware that you need at least $25,000 in your account to avoid trading restrictions in the US. This is the "pattern day trading" rule.

Select a Broker

Once you obtain sufficient capital to open an account, you should research brokers. Much like a supermarket stocking 100 cereals from a dozen different manufacturers, the stock brokerage industry has many players and options. Each broker offers many account types.

To make things simpler, I suggest you first list all the account attributes that are important to you. You list could look like this:

* Minimum amount to open account

* Monthly fees
* Margin rates (should you trade with margin)
* Short selling restrictions (should you want to sell stock short-an advanced contrarian topic)
* Mobile/Desktop app features
* Research-availability and costs
* Broker reputation-sanctions, fines, complaints
* Commission rates
* Ease of adding and withdrawing money
* Professional advice and stock picks

You will not find all criteria important. In addition, you will develop additional criteria. A few hours of research, though, should lead you to a few good broker choices.

Some of the most popular US brokers include:

TD Ameritrade-www.tdameritrade.com
Vanguard-www.vanguard.com
Charles Schwab-www.schwab.com
Fidelity-www.fidelity.com
Interactive Brokers-www.interactivebrokers.com
Tradestation-www.TradeStation.com
E*Trade-www.etrade.com
Merrill Edge-www.merrilledge.com
Robinhood-www.robinhood.com

This is a good starting list. All brokers have advantages and disadvantages. The superior choice will be different for everyone. I personally have had, or currently have, accounts with 6 of the brokers on this list.

Open and Fund Account

Once you select a broker, you simply go to their website and fill out an application. Once approved, you will be given instructions on funding your new account.

What About Zero Commissions?

In the past few years, the landscape of stock trading has really changed. What used to cost money is now free! But is it really? Let's take a look...

Back when I started trading with Charles Schwab, back in the late 1980's, you had to pay commissions to buy and sell stock. Charles Schwab was considered a "discount" broker, and the commission charge was somewhere in the $10-$30 range per trade. That commission charge was fairly hefty for small accounts, and it really made you think before executing a trade.

Maybe it wasn't so smart, but I remember sometimes not wanting to buy or sell a stock because of the commission charge. Maybe I should have focused instead on the expected stock movement instead!

Fast forward to today, and $0 commissions on stock trades are the norm. How can brokerages survive without charging fees? Well, don't worry about them. They sell your trade information to hedge funds and others who use your buy/sell data.   They also make money off of advisory services and other products. Finally, brokerages make money from lending out deposited (customer) money, and they make money from interest on margin account loans.

The point is that brokerages can survive by offering retail traders $0 commissions, although to be honest I have noticed a decrease in customer service at some brokerages after implementing this practice.

How has $0 commissions changed the competitive landscape? I'll discuss this a bit later when I write about GameStop and the rise of the Millenials as an investing group, but things have really changed in the past few years.

For many new players, I think trading and investing in stocks is more gambling now, and that is not necessarily a good thing.

Gambling in the financial markets is bad, but trading and investing can be good.

Start Trading

If you've made it this far, you are now ready to start trading! We'll discuss stock selection later, but for now, let's just assume you know what you are going to purchase.

Most brokers allow you to call in orders, but in this computer age, most traders simply enter the order on the broker's website or their mobile app.

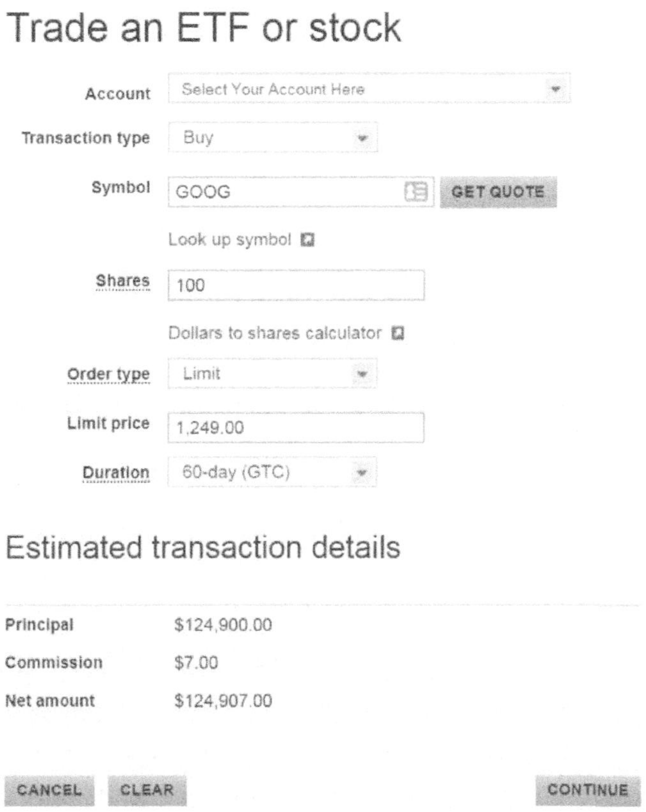

Trade an ETF or stock

Account	Select Your Account Here
Transaction type	Buy
Symbol	GOOG GET QUOTE
	Look up symbol
Shares	100
	Dollars to shares calculator
Order type	Limit
Limit price	1,249.00
Duration	60-day (GTC)

Estimated transaction details

Principal	$124,900.00
Commission	$7.00
Net amount	$124,907.00

CANCEL   CLEAR   CONTINUE

Figure 2-Vanguard's Order Entry Screen

9

Since every broker's order entry screen will be different, I won't describe any particular broker's setup. Instead, I will just explain the major selections to make:

Account: If you have multiple accounts, you have to select one to fund this trade.

Transaction Type:
BUY-if you are buying the stock (opening a new position)
SELL-if you are selling the stock (closing the position)
SELL SHORT-If you are shorting a stock (an advanced technique), you will want to SELL SHORT to initiate a short position
BUY TO COVER-this will close a short position, leaving you flat

Symbol: The stock ticker symbol. Trading platforms typically have a lookup feature to assist with this.

Shares: The number of shares you want to purchase/sell. Some platforms let you enter a dollar amount rather than a share quantity.

Order Type: There are 4 primary order types. They are described below.

Market: Once submitted, this order will immediately execute at the best available price. If being long is more important than price, use this order.

Limit: If price is your primary concern, enter a price below the current market price when buying. Then, if price continues to fall, and it touches or goes below your limit price, you will receive a fill. Note that you are only guaranteed a fill if the stock price goes below your limit price. If the market price only touches your limit price, you may or may not get filled.

Stop: This is usually an exit order, although you can use it for entry, too. It is frequently referred to as a "stop loss." Say you own stock at $100 per share. Your analysis suggests that if the stock falls to $99, you do not want to own it. In this case, you'd put in an order to sell at $99 on a stop. Note that due to market conditions, your order could execute at a price worse than $99. There is no guarantee your fill will be at $99.

Stop Limit: This is a stop order, with an added condition. Using the above example, let's say you want a sell stop at $99, but if the market instantly drops from $100 to below $95, you do not want the stop order to fill at anything worse than $95. In this case, you will enter an order to sell on $99 on a stop, with a limit of $95. This might protect you during a violent, but temporary, price crash.

Duration: Time the order is in effect:

Day: The order is active for the current trading session only.

GTC: The order is active until it is canceled by you. Some brokers limit this to 30 or 60 days, and some brokers allow you to enter an expiration date.

At this point, you have an account open, and you know how to enter and exit trades. The next question (and the most important question) is: how do I figure out what to buy? That is addressed in the following chapters.

CHAPTER 3–KNOW YOURSELF FIRST

Later in Chapter 4, we will discuss the different types of stock available, and the primary methods for making buy and sell decisions for your portfolio. Regardless what your portfolio looks like, you must first know your destination.

Know Your Goals and Objectives First

In 2001, my wife and I honeymooned in France. Neither of us could speak French. Nevertheless we decided to visit Paris and the northern part of the country. To accomplish this, we had to rent a car, and in the pre-GPS days, we needed a paper map. We obtained maps from our local library before the trip. We succeeded in having a great time, because we had a goal (visit beautiful France) and a plan (rent a car, use borrowed maps).

The same idea holds true as you embark on your stock buying adventure. You need goals and a plan to reach them. Without both, you likely will wander aimlessly through the countryside.

So, you first need a goal for investing in stocks. What is your objective? Is it to pay for your baby's college 18 years from now? Or perhaps it is to provide you with a nice, stable retirement income?

Everyone will have different objectives. That will influence stocks you examine. Utility stocks are nice, for example, but they may not provide enough capital appreciation for someone saving for the future.

Therefore, like anything in life worth achieving, you need to set goals and objectives. Take some time, and figure out exactly where you want to end up with your stock investments. These questions can help you determine just that:

What kinds of return are you looking for, compared to the overall market?

If your goal is just to match the overall market, your investing plan will be completely different from someone with a desire to exceed the average by a large percentage. If you set the baseline as the market average, and compare everything to that, it will help you immensely in figuring out the best investing approach.

One word of caution: don't base your goals for an annual return from what you see on the Internet, especially Twitter. It seems like everyone on Twitter is getting 100-1000% annual returns on their money, doing it in their spare time, and doing it soooo easily.

99% guaranteed these returns are lies. (A good debunking source is https://www.twitter.com/guruleaks1) Sure, it is possible to earn over 100% per year (I did it 3 consecutive years in a real money, verified account with futures), but many times that comes with enormous risk. The simple fact is very few traders or investors get those kinds of returns.

My advice is to try to aim for average market returns at the low end, and 1.25 to 1.5 times market average on the high. So, if the market average is 15%, you'd aim for 19-23% annual returns. While this does not seem like much of a difference, at the end of 15 years, you'll have twice as much money from earning 20% annually compared to 15%. It adds up!

How much risk are you willing to endure?

Ask the average person what they are looking to achieve by stock investing, and chances are they'll mention an annual return percentage or dollar amount. Rarely, if ever, will they mention how much risk they are willing to accept to achieve that return.

Return and risk are highly correlated: if you want higher returns, you generally have to accept higher risk. There is no free lunch here; you cannot get unlimited returns with zero risk.

Think of your bank account. Your account balance never goes down, so in that sense you are risking nothing (in reality there is currency risk, inflation risk, bank failure risk, government confiscation risk, government collapse risk and more, but those risks are best discussed elsewhere). For this "zero" risk, though, you get a very small return-currently a 0-2% interest rate.

Risk can be measured in different ways, but for this book, I'll use drawdown as our risk measure. Drawdown is simply the amount of loss endured from the last equity peak. For example, during a year if your account starts at $10,000, reaches a peak of $15,000 and ends the year at a new low of $12,500, you will have achieved a return of 25% 12,500/10,000 with a maximum drawdown of 17% (1-12,500/15,000). Your return to drawdown ratio is 25/17, or 1.47, which is very good.

As with annual return, the risk can be compared to the market average. The important point is to know up front how much risk you are willing to endure.

What is your time horizon for investing?

If you are 65 and retired, chances are investing in emerging technology that may not pay off for 10-20 years is not for you. By the same token, a 25-year-old with 40 years to invest might not want to be concentrated in low growth dividend stocks. So, the time you have to invest should be a consideration in your stock selection.

Generally, the more time you have, the more risks you can take, since you'll have more time for your approach to become profitable. The younger you are, the more likely you will be to find growth stocks to be appropriate. My middle school-age children, who I'll discuss later in the case studies section, are a perfect example of growth stock investors. They have a lifetime of stock investing ahead of them, so growth stocks are a good choice.

How much time are you willing to dedicate to studying the stock market?

The final question you need to address is also time related, but does not refer to your investment time horizon. Instead, this question is about the time you can "invest" in your stock investing project. With a full time career or full time school, you can't dedicate 40+ hours per week to study the stock market. Maybe 5-15 hours per week is possible instead. If you work 70-80 hours a week, you might not even carve out that much time.

Recognizing your time availability will definitely impact the stock investing road you choose. If you know this upfront, you won't waste time pursuing an approach that takes too much of your time.

To help you out, later in the book when I discuss specific stock investing levels, I'll include the following criteria, which you can compare to your goals and objectives:

Expected Annual Return
Expected Risk
Time Horizon
Expected Time Commitment

That way, for each investing approach, you can pick the approach or tier that best matches your goals.

CHAPTER 4-STOCKS, CATEGORIZED

Before I jump into some potential approaches for your stock investing journey, it is important to discuss a few more basics. The first deals with the different types of stocks. The second area discusses a few different approaches to analyzing stocks. Since both of these play into your investment goals and objectives, it is important to discuss them before we get into the investment plan details. In this chapter, we'll discuss stock categories.

Major Categories of Stocks

There are different flavors of stocks, just like there are different companies and industries. Some companies grow quickly, and other are slow and steady. Each one has its pros and cons, and each one can be valuable to your stock portfolio. Where it gets tricky is that many stocks fall into multiple categories. For example, a growth stock can also be a dividend producing stock. Putting that aside, lets first look at major categories of stocks, and reasons to invest in each.

I'll first start with a special category of stocks, the ETFs. ETF stands for Exchange Traded Fund, and is basically a stock of other stocks. Buying the SPY ETF (The SPDR S&P500 Trust ETF), for example, actually gives you exposure to all the stocks in the S&P 500. You don't actually own any of the S&P500 stocks, but the Trust does. So, this ETF tracks S&P500 performance, providing much of the diversification without the hassle of owning 500 different stocks.

At last count, there are over 5,000 ETF stocks you can buy. They cover a wide range of industries, investment styles, and also serve a wide range of purposes. The biggest benefit of ETFs is that you can benefit from diversification a lot easier than buying individual stocks.

For instance, say you want to invest in a legal marijuana company. Which should you choose? It may take a lot of research to determine which one to buy. Instead you could buy the cannabis ETF (aptly named) TOKE. This would give you exposure to the whole cannabis industry, without the risk of picking the wrong company.

Another benefit is that ETFs have pretty low management fees, especially compared to actively managed mutual funds. This sways many people to choose ETFs over mutual funds. In fact, the trend is clear. More people are investing in ETFs every year, and soon ETF investment will surpass mutual fund investment. Why pay a manager big fees for actively managing a mutual fund portfolio? Instead you could have a passive ETF with comparable performance and lower fees.

Indexing on the Rise
Passive U.S. equity funds could soon overtake their active peers

■ Active   ■ Passive

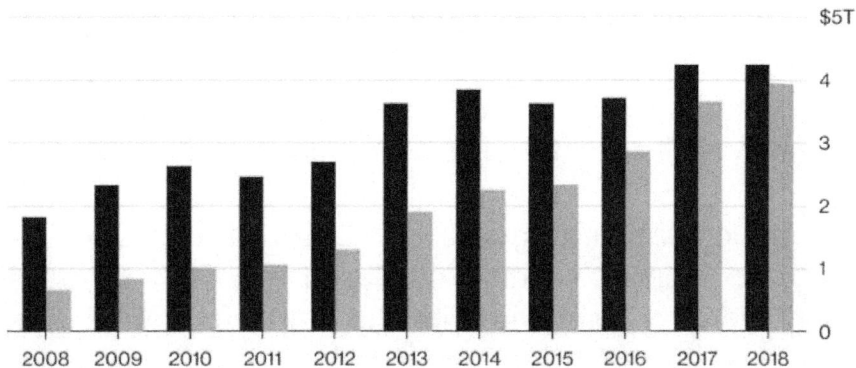

Source: Morningstar Inc.
Note: 2018 data as of Nov. 30

https://www.bloomberg.com/news/articles/2018-12-31/shift-from-active-to-passive-approaches-tipping-point-in-2019

Figure 3- Soon ETF Investments Will Surpass Mutual Fund Investments

17

It should be pretty clear that ETFs can save you a lot of time and stress compared to picking individual stocks. But let's say you still want to select individual stocks. The first thing you should identify is the stock type. Stocks are generally identified in one of the following categories (but keep in mind, a stock may fit in more than one category).

Value stocks

Value stocks are generally considered "good deals." One way to think about it is buying something worth $10, but only paying $8 for it. For various reasons, investors do not value the stock as much as they should. It could have a lower price than comparable stocks in its industry, and it may have a stock price that does not reflect the company's true value.

The trick with value stocks is finding ones where the long-term prospects (ie, appreciation) are not reflected in the current price. If you get in before the market prices the stock appropriately, then you will benefit.

Dividend stocks

Some stocks return cash to investors at regular intervals. These returns are dividends, and can be a significant component of the stock's overall return. Even if the stock price remains flat, it might pay an annual dividend rate of 5%, which could make it worth holding.

There is a popular strategy called "Dogs of The Dow" where investors buy the highest yielding stocks in the Dow Jones. Each year, the portfolio is rebalanced with the 5 to 10 highest dividend yield stocks. This approach incorporates both dividend stocks and value stocks, since undervalued stocks tend to have a higher dividend.

Growth stocks

A growth stock is, just as its name implies, a stock in a corporation where revenues and earnings (profits) are rising. Many companies in this regime are young, fast growing, and higher risk. An example is first movers in a sector.

If you are a long-term investor, growth stocks should definitely be in your portfolio.

Penny stocks

Some stocks trade at a very low price. Penny stocks is the common term for them. Companies in this sector may be great, but small, companies. Or, they can be very risky, poorly run companies. Many penny stocks are sold via "pink sheets"-the stock is too small to be listed on a major exchange, so they are listed on the OTC (over the counter) market.

Penny stocks can also be manipulated by unscrupulous concerns. A common tactic is for a newsletter writer to buy a penny stock, then recommend it to his followers. The demand of the followers causes the price to rise, and the newsletter owner sells his shares to his readers at a profit. Later, when the demand for the stock dies down, the price falls back down, leaving the readers with a losing stock.

You will see many Internet ads for penny stocks; some people do very well with them. Most people, though, should avoid penny stocks.

Blue Chip Stocks

Blue chip stocks are considered the best companies to buy stock in. This does not mean they will provide the best returns, but many times they provide a more stable return to risk characteristics. Blue chips are big, established companies here for the long haul. Wal-Mart (WMT) is a good example of a blue chip stock.

One way to think about blue chips is that they are companies you would tell your grandma to invest in. Safe and stable is the goal here.

New Stocks-Initial Public Offerings (IPOs)

In any economy, new companies are continually being born. In the beginning, company ownership includes the founders, some initial investors and possibly some venture capital firms. Eventually these groups will "cash out." They do this by offering stock to the public, via an Initial Public Offering (IPO).

For the typical retail trader, the only way to take part in an IPO is after public trading actually starts. Unfortunately, many times the stock price jumps the first day of trading, and latecomers miss out on the initial run up. If long term performance of the company is acceptable, this is not usually a problem. But some companies peak at the IPO, and their stock price never really increases after that.

Since the companies offering IPOs are generally fairly new, there is higher risk in these stocks. Some IPOs succeed, however some crash and burn. How do you know which is which? You don't, so one alternative might be to invest in an IPO ETF, which will then buy many of the IPOs offered.

Stocks By Sector/Industry

Just as you can define stocks by the type of company they are, you can also group stocks into different sectors or industries. There are important reasons why this is important. First, it is desirable to have a diversified portfolio. This means you own stocks in a number of different industries. Diversification helps limit your risk, although in bad times almost all stocks are likely to decline in value.

A second reason sector investing is important is because you can skew the portfolio balance to what you feel is best for the long term. For example, if you believe health care costs will continue to rise as the population ages, you might want to have more health care stocks. On the other hand, if you think government is going to put price caps on drugs and medical procedures, conceivably you want less exposure to this sector.

Some major sectors are listed below:

Energy
Raw Materials
Industrials
Consumer Discretionary
Consumer Staples
Health Care
Financials
Information Technology

When you combine the sectors with the types of stocks, you can see that the number of choices becomes overwhelming. How many Health Care growth stocks do you want? What about Financial dividend stocks? And don't forget Energy value stocks!

When you look at things this way, stock picking becomes daunting, and the myriad of choices can actually be paralyzing. It becomes so hard to decide that no decision is ever made.

My advice: don't worry about covering every sector or every stock type. Instead, focus on finding good companies, no matter the type of stock or the industry. Concurrently, check that all your eggs are in multiple baskets. Having all energy stocks, for instance, is good at times, but usually is not.

With my advice of finding good companies, that then becomes the next question: just how do you define good companies, and more importantly, how do you actually find them? And once you do, when do you enter trades? I discuss all that in the next chapter by introducing fundamental and technical analysis and the types of trading.

CHAPTER 5-ANALYZING AND TRADING STOCKS, UTILIZING RISK CAPITAL

Types of Analysis

At this point, let's say you know you want to pick a growth stock from the technology sector. After doing some research, let's say you've decided on Facebook (FB) as the stock you want to buy. What do you do next? How do you actually determine if it is worth buying, and when is the best time to buy it? The answers are found in fundamental and technical analysis.

Fundamental

Price to earnings ratio. Book value. Net income. EBITDA. Annual report footnotes.

If all these terms sound foreign to you, don't feel bad. You are definitely not alone. These financial terms, and hundreds more, are used to quantify the financial condition of companies. These numbers are analyzed and dissected with what is commonly called fundamental analysis.

If you want to investigate the financial situation of a company before you buy its stock, you will perform some sort of fundamental analysis or due diligence. This goes beyond watching the company CEO speak on CNBC. It involves a lot of work. In fact, thousands are employed by brokerages and trading firms to study annual reports in the quest for finding good stocks.

The problem is that this analysis can quickly become overwhelming. How much analysis is required before you conclude a stock is worthwhile or not? What numbers are important, or not?

The scope of fundamental analysis goes far beyond this book. If this kind of stock analysis intrigues you, I suggest one or more of the following books:

"Security Analysis: Sixth Edition" by Benjamin Graham (considered the bible of fundamental analysis)

"How to Make Money in Stocks: A Winning System in Good Times and Bad" by William J. O'Neil (introduces the CAN SLIM method of using fundamental analysis to pick stocks)

"The Intelligent Investor: The Definitive Book on Value Investing. A Book of Practical Counsel," by Benjamin Graham (another fundamental investing classic)

Of course, once you pinpoint a few fundamental metrics, you will need to calculate the values for every stock in order to see which stocks have good numbers. Finviz (https://finviz.com/screener.ashx) has an excellent stock screener for both fundamental and technical factors. Many brokerages are provide tools to assist in this regard. These screeners make your selection job a lot easier.

Technical

Technical Analysis is an alternative to poring over annual reports. It assumes that all information about a company is already reflected in the stock price. For example, if the investing world thinks, after examining the company's annual report, that prospects for future growth are likely, then the price of the stock should rise.

Using technical analysis, there is no need for the investor to examine the financial books. Many others have already done that. That consensus opinion gets reflected in the stock price. This certainly simplifies things!

The problem is that technical analysis is wrong many times and sometimes goes off in crazy directions. The stock price of Enron and all its technical indicators looked great for a long time, for instance, as the investing world concluded its financial condition was sound. Then it collapsed with little technical warning, as the underlying fundamentals of the company were fraudulent.

Technical analysis primarily uses the stock price itself to determine if the stock is worth buying. One example is if the price is above its 50 day moving average, the stock is in a bull trend, and is appropriate to buy.

Moving averages are probably the simplest example of technical analysis. Just like fundamental analysis, the numbers get a lot more complicated as you dig deeper into it. More complicated technical analysis techniques include Fibonacci analysis, Elliott wave theory, overbought and oversold indicators and Gann charts. Some investors swear by these methods. Other investors swear AT them.

Figure 4- Typical Technical Analysis On A Price Chart

Just as with fundamentals, the field of technical analysis is huge, and has thousands of supporters. For the interested reader, excellent books on technical analysis include:

"Technical Analysis of the Financial Markets: A Comprehensive Guide to Trading Methods and Applications," by John Murphy

"Charting and Technical Analysis," by Fred McAllen

Combination

Of course, you do not have to be strictly a fundamental trader, or a technical analyst. You can incorporate both into your stock selection process. Personally, I like to use a little fundamental analysis to first screen stocks. As an example, I like stocks where the earnings of the company have been steadily increasing (fundamental) and the stock price is above its 50 day moving average (technical). While this doesn't mean the stock price will continue to increase indefinitely, at least right now it seems like the company is doing something right.

The aforementioned stock screening tools help you with fundamental and technical screening. For example, you could ask the tool to give you every stock trading at $X or more, with increasing earnings the last 3 quarters, with a stock price below its book value, that is not overbought according to technical criteria. In a few seconds, you'd have a list of stocks meeting that criteria.

Once I see that simple fundamental and technical analysis look acceptable, I'll then look at the stock price chart and do some simple analysis. If the recent stock price has been headed down, with fundamental earnings per share going up, alarm bells go off in my head. Possibly everyone else is wrong, and they don't realize how great the company is. More likely, holes exist in my quick analysis. For example, a new competitor moving into the field might lead to a stock price drop, even though earnings numbers looked acceptable. While earnings of the company were historically good, with more competition perhaps future prospects are poor. The best stock picks have technical and fundamental analysis aligned.

The degree you use one, both or neither of these evaluation methods depends in part on how you plan to trade the stock. A day trader-an investor who holds the stock for a few minutes-probably does not care about the fundamentals. A long-term investor, on the other hand, probably does not care about a short term dip in stock price (in fact, she may look at the dip not as a bad sign, but as an even greater buying opportunity).

So, your use of fundamental and/or technical analysis will depend on your trading/investing style. That is covered below.

Types of Trading

As I mentioned previously, the type of analysis you will do for your stock buying and selling decisions will depend in part on how you are going to trade. As with other areas of stock investing, there are many nuanced ways to trade. To keep things simple, I am going to discuss only 3 of the most popular methods: day trading, active long term trading and passive long term trading. The last one is really considered investing, as opposed to traditional "trading" (which is usually a shorter term duration).

Day Trading

Picture yourself sitting in your pajamas in front of your computer, clicking charts and order forms frenetically, hearing the cash register ring with each successful trade. Or, you are lounging on the beach, your brokerage app active on your phone as you tap the buy and sell buttons in between sips from your giant margarita glass.

Most people envision day trading that way. Successful traders rapidly buying and selling, eventually becoming massively profitable after each day of clicking or tapping away. Some people do just this. For most day traders, however, it is a losing battle. Sorry to burst your bubble!

But what exactly is day trading? In its simplest form, it is just buying and selling a stock in the same day, sometimes entering and exiting within minutes or even seconds. This approach depends on simple technical analysis, trader intuition and many times a bit of luck. Money management is also a key component for a good day trader. Fundamental analysis does not really play a role in day trading, unless there is a news announcement or earnings report.

Day traders typically rely on price charts or the order book to make split-second decisions. They might also write computer programs (algorithms, or algos) to automate trading. With an algo, they can trade many stocks simultaneously.

Day trading was very popular in the tech boom of the late 1990s, and many fortunes were made (and later lost) by day traders. Eventually, though, the market adjusted to all these traders, and currently day trading is a lot harder than it used to be.

For >95% of population, stock day trading is NOT appropriate. Long term investing is a superior choice.

Long Term Trading

While day trading might be appropriate for a select few, long term trading is probably the best choice for individuals wanting to invest in stocks for the long term. By long term I mean months/years of investing. In that case, trades can last for days, weeks, months, years or even decades.

Active Long Term Trading

If you plan on regularly checking your portfolio and making adjustments, you are considered an active long term trader. Perhaps you review your stock performance every month and make changes to your portfolio. Or, you create a simple algorithm that trades for you, based on a daily/weekly chart.

The key here is you are making trading decisions based not of movements during the day, but rather on weekly or monthly variations. Most stock investors fall into this category. They take trades infrequently, but at the same time they do not ignore their portfolio. They are "in the game."

Passive Long Term Trading

Passive long term investing is ideal for retirement accounts. It is also appropriate for those without the time or inclination for active trading. An example is buying Wal-Mart and holding for the next 20 years.

Passive investing like this is akin to "set it and forget it." You assume that over the long term, stocks will go up, and just as a rising tide raises all ships, your stock should also rise along with the overall market.

Of course, this approach can be dangerous if the individual stocks you choose fail or go bankrupt. So, this passive approach is best done via broad market ETFs. As long as the general market goes up, so should the general market ETFs.

Your time horizon for passive long term investing should be anything over 10 years. That is why it is ideal for retirement accounts. Buy some SPY ETF stock in your 20s, and you should have a nice nest egg by the time you turn 50 or 60. That will hold if the economy continues to perform.

Trading Capital-Getting Your Financial House In Order

So far, we have explored the basics of stock investing. We have learned about why we should invest, established the different types of stocks, discovered the major methods of evaluating stocks and discussed the different approaches to trading.

Before I get into specific details on different investing "tiers," it is important to discuss the role of stock investing in your overall financial health. After all, without money to invest, you can't play in the stock market!

Risk Capital

If you recall, early on I explained that stock investing should only utilize risk capital. This is money you can afford to lose, without it impacting your current lifestyle. The question is: how do you acquire risk capital?

Assuming you did not have a rich uncle who left you millions, or you did not receive a settlement, like I did, from a dog who treated your face like a chew toy (in retrospect, I should have invested my dog bite money in the stock market for 30 years, and not bought a fancy sports car instead), you have to obtain risk capital the old fashioned way-by saving for it.

A good rule of thumb is to save 10% of your income. This small amount adds up over time. If you make $50,000 per year, after 10 years you'll end up with $50,000 to invest, which is a significant sum.

When told to save 10% of their income, most people just scoff. "How can I afford fancy dinners, or nights out on the town, when I have to save that much?" they exclaim. I agree, saving 10% is hard to do in this instant "I want it now" world. Most people eschew delaying the good life; they want to live large right now.

So, putting 10% of your money aside for investing becomes a lifestyle choice. You will have to give up something today, in the hopes of potentially having a lot more money in the future. It is what responsible, forward thinking people do.

In fact, many people have started going well beyond 10% savings. Just google "Financial Independence, Retire Early" (F.I.R.E) to learn more about a growing movement where people save 50-80% of their current income. These extreme savers live frugally in the hopes of retiring very early.

If you are trying to figure out how you can do this, you might have already realized you need a budget. Tracking expenditures is key. By doing this, you can figure out areas where you are wasting money. I have tracked my spending for my whole adult life, and it has helped me save money and avoid frivolous expenses.

To some of you, this discussion is probably a real downer. You make money, and you want to spend it however you want. How dare some author tell you to watch what you spend! Well, most people live for today. Consequently, they have no money or savings in old age. What happens then? Many of these people live on ramen noodles and rice cakes in their old age and rely on their children to support them. Not a good outcome.

Budgeting, saving and planning for the future is all about being a responsible adult. It is the smart path.

One important additional point is that having credit card debt will just defeat the purpose of saving 10%. Don't try to supplement your lifestyle by using credit cards. Smart people use credit cards, but pay off the balance in full each month. It makes no sense to save 10% of your income, only to rack up credit card debt that will cost you 20% in annual interest.

When compared to F.I.R.E. advocates, saving 10% annually is not that extreme, and will not have a major impact on your current lifestyle.   With that 10% yearly savings, you can invest for your future with stocks.

This 10% rule is also a great rule to teach your children and gives them solid savings habits at an early age. If they get a $10 allowance, take $1 out as you give it to them, and explain it is dedicated to savings. My friend Ken did that with his kids. He even deducted more for taxes. He provided a nice, sobering lesson in reality for his kids!

If your children get a part-time job, make them put at least 10% of the gross earnings in a savings account. A small amount, yet an enormous long term lesson.

In summing up, you need risk capital to invest in stocks, and that should come from a properly managed overall financial situation. Save 10% of your income, stay within your budget and avoid credit card debt. You'll then be in an ideal position for stock investing.

CHAPTER 6-INTRODUCING STOCK INVESTING TIERS-THE STOCK PICKING PYRAMID

Up to this point, I have covered some basics, the foundation if you will, to proper stock investing:

Why Stocks Are A Good Investment
Exactly What Stocks Are
Getting Money To Invest With
Selecting A Broker
Trading Basics
Different Types of Stocks
Fundamental Analysis
Technical Analysis
Different Types of Trading
Getting Your Financial House In Order

With those foundation pieces in place, I'll now explore different tiers of stocks investing. I call them tiers, levels or steps on a pyramid because the approach I lay out is based on the amount of time and the amount of effort you put into stock investing. At the lowest level, the time and effort is minimal. At the highest tier, the time and effort is significant.

Figure 5- The Stock Market Picking Pyramid

One level (or more) is just right for your circumstances. Many people invest at multiple levels.

For each tier, before describing it, I'll categorize it relative to the 4 goals and objectives I described earlier:

Potential Returns—Relative to the stock market as a whole, what kind of performance (returns) are you looking for? Are you looking to match the market, or possibly wildly exceed it?

Risk Profile—Again relative to the general market, how much risk are you willing to accept? Do you want your stock investments to be less risky than the overall market? Or conversely, are you willing to risk it all in the hopes of big gains?

Time Horizon—Are you investing in stocks to purchase a house in a few years, or are you willing to wait for 10-30 years for your investment to pay off?

Time Commitment—How much time on a daily or weekly basis are you willing to spend working on your stocks? Will it be like a hobby, a part-time job or a full-time job for you? If you have a demanding full time career, you'll definitely be at a different level than a retiree who is willing to spend 40 hours a week analyzing the stock market.

A couple of important points to remember regarding the investing tiers. First, no tier is superlative. I have seen people succeed at each level of the pyramid. Unfortunately, I have also seen people miserably fail at each tier. Time invested at higher tiers does NOT guarantee a better return. At higher tiers, it is entirely possible you will do worse than those at lower tiers, especially after you consider the amount of time you have to dedicate at the higher levels.

Another important point is that you don't have to relegate yourself to one tier. For example, with my retirement accounts, I invest based on the lower tiers. At the same time, I also invest some money at the higher tiers, by developing algorithms to trade with.

Finally, the tiers can be used sequentially if you so choose. You might start out today with the lowest tier, and you might find you enjoy stock investing. Then, you'll naturally spend more time watching your investments, and progress to a higher tier. The neat thing is the decision is all in your hands-you can be in charge of your financial future. The real key is to get started, and start investing, as soon as you are able.

Tier 1-Buy The Market
Tier 2-Follow Broker, Newsletter or Other Recommendations
Tier 3-Follow The Legends
Tier 4-Build Your Own ETFs or Mutual Fund Portfolio
Tier 5-Pick Your Own Stocks-Simple Version
Tier 6-Adding a Market Timer to Your Approach
Tier 7-Build Your Own Stock Picker/Trader Algo
Tier 8-Exotic Approaches-Options, Shorting Stock and More

With that background established, let's look at the different tiers of the Stock Picking Pyramid.

CHAPTER 7-TIER 1-BUY THE MARKET

> **TIER 1-Buy The Market**
> **Potential Returns**-Market average
> **Risk Profile**-Market average
> **Time Horizon**-Medium To Long Term
> **Time Commitment**-Minimal

Think back to your days in school. Along with the fond memories and the painful episodes, remember how you and your family always wanted you to get good grades? If you were like me, your goal was always to be the best-to get an A. Getting straight A's was an accomplishment worth striving for. With an A, you were doing well.

Conversely, if you were average, you received a C (which these days has been inflated to a B or B-). No one wanted to be just average!

For many stock investors, that "get an A" mentality spills over into their stock picking. They want to be the best. The problem is, it is really hard to be the best, and even if you are in any given year, it is really hard to stay at the top year after year.

You would think professional investors are at the top. After all, their job is to outperform the market through their superior stock picking skills. Yet, according to an S&P Dow Jones Indices report, in 2018 a majority of 64.5% of large capitalization mutual fund managers underperformed the market.

It gets even worse. Over a 10-year period, 85% of these managers underperformed the market, and over 15 years the

underperformers numbered 92%.
https://www.cnbc.com/2019/03/15/active-fund-managers-trail-the-sp-500-for-the-ninth-year-in-a-row-in-triumph-for-indexing.html

Now, you might argue that these fund managers have to be paid, so their compensation has to lower the returns to clients. Frequently top performers attract more money under management, but more assets to manage can reduce performance.

Whatever the reasons, the bottom line is this: professionals have a tough time beating the market average. How does that impact you and me?

First, it should tell you that superior investing is a tough job. Second, maybe-just maybe-when it comes to investing in the stock market, achieving average performance is not all that bad. In fact, Tier 1 is all about being average.

Tier 1 investing then becomes really simple: just buy the SPY ETF, which is the basket of stocks in the S&P500. You'll achieve the average market return, with the same risk as the market (actually, your returns will be a tiny bit lower than the S&P500 average, due to administrative costs, etc.). For the SPY, you are actually investing in the 500 stocks that make up the S&P500, so it technically is not the whole market of 3000-4000 stocks available in the US, but it is a well-diversified cross section of the overall market. It is average performance and easy to do.

Being average is not all that bad. Over a long period, the S&P 500 has returned between 8-10% annually, depending on the time period you look at. That certainly is good-with this, you'll roughly double your money every 7-10 years. If you start doing this when you are 25 by investing $10,000, by the time you are 65 you could have $200,000 or more. Not too shabby!

Tier 1 is the perfect approach for people satisfied in achieving the overall market average. True, you will be a bore at cocktail parties bragging about your average performance, but you can sleep soundly knowing you are beating most people out there.

Tier 1 is also perfect for people with little time for market analysis. Why waste time chasing an "A" when very, very few people achieve it? Of course, that challenge compels people to try. Such challenges are best avoided by most.

Finally, even if you focus on the higher tiers, set aside at least some of your funds for this level. Then, no matter how poorly (or good) you do with the other tiers, you can relax knowing a chunk of your savings is at least reaching average performance levels.

<u>Sample Implementation - Tier 1</u>
Buy General Market ETFs

SPY – S&P500 Index
QQQ – Nasdaq 100 Index
IWM – Russell 2000 Index
DIA – Dow Jones Industrial Average Index

CHAPTER 8-TIER 2-FOLLOW BROKER, NEWSLETTER OR OTHER RECOMMENDATIONS

<u>TIER 2-Follow 3rd Party Recommendations</u>
Potential Returns-Above average
Risk Profile-Above average
Time Horizon-All horizons
Time Commitment-Moderate

Your brother-in-law looks around, suspiciously eyeing the nearby crowd milling around at the dinner party. Seeing no one is watching, he whispers to you "I've got a hot tip on Spacely Sprocket stock. My cousin is friends with the person who dog walks for the assistant to the CEO of the company. The CEO, Mr. Spacely, is going to China for a month on a top secret trip, and is closing on a big deal to manufacture plastic polymer sprockets. When news becomes public, the stock is going sky high! Let's get rich! Gimme a fist bump, bruh!"

Perhaps you believe your brother-in-law, or instead you think he is full of it. If he is telling the truth, yes you could make money, but also yes, you could get nabbed for illegal insider trading. And if he is full of it, as most brothers-in-law many times are, investing in his scheme will only cost you money.

But, if you are in the stock game, recommendations are just part of the adventure. These recommendations come from sources good and also sources bad. For this tier, recommendations will help you pick individual stocks, although you could also use tips to select ETFs for whole industries.

Let's look at these recommendations and see how you can effectively use them.

Broker Recommendations

Most brokers have a research arm, which will provide you with "hot" stocks. Even in a bear market-where almost every stock is falling-the broker will still have plenty of great stocks (according to them) for you to buy. That is amusing (and concerning).

Once you realize that the broker's job is to get you to buy stocks, you'll understand their bias. Now, possibly they will be right. Many times they are, and many brokerages provide good advice. You just have to be careful.

One way to protect yourself (and this also holds for newsletter and other recommendations) is to track the recommendations. Set up a simple spreadsheet with the stock pick, who made it, the entry price and the exit price. After doing this for a few months, you might discover who provides good stock picks, and who doesn't.

Newsletter Recommendations

If it seems like there are hundreds of people selling their stock picks via alerts or newsletters, you are right.   Stock picking advice via newsletters is a huge industry. The Hulbert Financial Digest (http://hulbertratings.com/12-month-scoreboard/) tracks only 117 newsletters, and that is just the tip of the iceberg. With prices running from $49 per year to over $10,000 per year, recommending stocks is big business.

The problem, as presented earlier, is if you want to go this route, it requires double tracking. First, you track the newsletters' picks. Then, you track the prices of the individual picks themselves. So, you are making a lot more decisions, and spending a lot of time not analyzing the stocks themselves. Instead, you analyze other people who are analyzing stocks!

My advice regarding newsletters: try to find verified records for the target newsletter.   Don't rely on just the newsletter writer's reported results. Many will "accidentally" have bad picks disappear, yet always include successful picks. But, this advice adds even more complexity. Now you have to research the ratings/track record verification service, who then analyzes the stock newsletter, who in turn analyzes the stock.

Talking Head Recommendations

Watch CNBC or Fox Business Channel for a while, and you will be astonished and amazed at the proclamations from both the anchors and the guests. "Wow!" you think, "these people are geniuses! I'll follow what they tell me." Many among us draw this conclusion.

Just remember these channels are ENTERTAINMENT. Their job is to keep you watching, and they will do or say anything to keep you tuned in. Some of their picks will pay off, and some will not. But if these shows give you a few ideas, and keep you exciting about stock investing, it could be worth your time.

A few years ago, the CXO group did a study, where they tracked over 6,000 stock picks made by over 65 guests. Now, if these guests just flipped a coin on each pick, they should have gotten 50% of the picks right. Well, guess what? As a group, they were correct on only 47% of calls!

Even the best stock picker was correct only 68%, and likely some of that was luck.

The point is these so-called experts can't predict the future. No one can. And if their aggregate track record is worse than flipping a coin, why should you even listen to them?

Twitter, Your Know-It-All Relatives and Other Shady Characters

When people find out you are an active stock trader, stock touters come out of the woodwork. Sign up for free stock information via e-mail, and you will receive phone calls about gold stocks, with hot tips from a pushy salesman. Smart money is selling low float (low volume) stocks to the unwary.

Friends and family will have opinions, too. I discuss my adventure in this realm later on, but for now realize that taking tips from family or friends can be a mistake. It is easy for them to throw out suggestions with no downside, since it is your money on the line. It the pick goes wrong, you'll never hear from them. But when the pick works out, you'll never hear the end of it.

Finally, there is a special place reserved in financial Hell for stock pickers on Twitter, or "fintwit" as it is also known. It is truly amazing-it seems like no stock picker on Twitter ever loses. Many times, the con works like this: the con artist stock picker opens a Twitter account, and posts a few stock picks. Successful tweets are repeated ad nauseam. The bad picks disappear, along with the tweets.   Over time, people follow this new stock picker with the great, time stamped record.

But the shenanigans don't stop there. The good con artists can mask the bad trades and invent good trades out of thin air. One common tactic is to find a stock that gapped up, and then tweet "I just exited my long at a big profit." Yet, there was never an initial tweet for the entry! You might think that is crazy. That it never works. Yet, you'd be shocked how many gullible people are suckered in.

Eventually, the stock picking "genius," with a nice timeline of time stamped tweets (a poor man's verification), will announce a premium stock pick service-with special picks allegedly even better than the free Twitter picks. And you can join in before the doors close. Lucky (unlucky?) you!

Summing Up Newsletters and Other Stock Pickers

I realize I've painted a bad picture of stock pickers, and I have probably been a bit unfair. I'm sure there are honest, decent, hardworking and ethical stock picking newsletter writers, talking heads, Twitter folk and brokerage research departments out there. And they need praise for the great job they do. There are also market experts who do a very good job forecasting the general market conditions.

But, most newsletter writers and other recommenders of stocks have just one motive-to take money out of your pocket. It might be thru sales commissions, newsletter fees or online premium services, but it will still cost you all the same.

So, if you pursue newsletters and advice for your stock picks, realize that you will spend a lot of time "picking the pickers." Maybe the time you'll spend analyzing the pickers would have been better spent picking your own stocks.

<u>Sample Implementation - Tier 2</u>

Always fully research stock ideas from these sources

<u>Newsletters</u>
Motley Fool Stock Advisor – fool.com
Zacks Investment Research – zacks.com
Kiplinger's Personal Finance – Kiplinger.com
Hulbert Ratings – hulbertratings.com

<u>TV Personalities</u>
Jim Cramer - CNBC Mad Money

CHAPTER 9-TIER 3-FOLLOW THE LEGENDS

Tier 3-Follow The Legends
Potential Returns-Above average
Risk Profile-Above average
Time Horizon-Long Term
Time Commitment-Small to Medium

This tier is a step up from newsletter writers and Twitter stock pickers. Instead of relying on recommendations from groups you may not trust, why not just follow what legendary investors do? It is hard to argue that mimicking the picks of billionaire Warren Buffett, for example, is a bad idea. He became a billionaire because of his stock buying and selling decisions. How many people can honestly say that?

Here are some investing billionaires who you will recognize:

Warren Buffett
Bill Gates
Carl Icahn
George Soros

They all became rich, stayed rich, and/or became richer through their investments. Sure, Bill Gates, the founder of Microsoft, did not pick stocks to become rich in the first place, but he definitely grew his wealth by making shrewd stock investments.

This tier then becomes pretty simple once you pick your billionaire. Just mimic stock portfolios of billionaires. The website https://www.theinvestorspodcast.com/legend-investors-stock-portfolio/ is great for this. Just click on Carl Icahn's face, and you'll see what stocks he is invested in. Pretty neat!

The tough part about this tier is that some billionaires own many stocks, and you will not be able to buy them all. One alternative is to randomly select a handful of their picks. This eliminates a bias on your end-the tendency to pick familiar stocks to you. Another option, at least for Warren Buffett, is just to invest in his company, Berkshire Hathaway (BRK.A and BRK.B). Doing so will basically replicate his stock portfolio. Interestingly enough, 50% of Bill Gates' portfolio is in Warren Buffett's BRK.B stock!

Obviously, there is no guarantee these individuals will continue to perform well, but given their proven wealth and proven track recorda, I certainly like their chances.

Sample Implementation – Tier 3
Follow Legends

Warren Buffett Top 5 Picks –AAPL, BAC, KO, WFC, AXP
Bill Gates Top 5 Picks – BRK.B, WM, CNI, CAT, WMT
Carl Icahn Top 5 Picks – IEP, CVI, OXY, HLF, LNG
Other Legends – https://www.theinvestorspodcast.com/legend-investors-stock-portfolio/

CHAPTER 10-TIER 4-BUILD YOUR OWN DIVERSIFIED ETF OR MUTUAL FUND PORTFOLIO

TIER 4-Build Your Own ETFs or Mutual Fund Portfolio
Potential Returns-Above average
Risk Profile-Above average
Time Horizon-Long Term
Time Commitment-Small to Medium

Earlier on, I discussed the benefits of diversification, and in a later chapter, I'll dig a little deeper into the topic. Diversification in the stock market is great, because it can insulate you from some bad stock picks. If you put all your money in one stock, and it crashes, you are in trouble. But, if you put your money in 10 stocks and 1 crashes, you will emerge bloody and bruised, but not completely crushed.

Exchange Traded Funds (ETFs) and their higher cost counterparts, actively managed mutual funds, take advantage of diversification. If you think the health care industry is going up, for example, why put all your money in one or two healthcare stocks-and risk them not doing well-when you can buy a basket of healthcare stocks via a targeted ETF?

ETFs and mutual funds provide market exposure, benefit from the general market rise, and minimize individual stock risk. Sure, you won't triple your money with the rare stock that suddenly surges, but you also will not be left holding the bag when your stock pick suddenly collapses.

The idea with tier 4 is to build your own portfolio of ETFs, based on where you see the world going. Remember my story about my mom and the dog bite settlement? Back when she banked the dog bite blood money, she was ignorant about stock market investing. But fast forward a few years, and she slowly became very good at selecting mutual funds (lower priced ETFs were not readily available back then). How did she do it?

My mom realized that individual stock picking (Tier 5) was not for her. Without a finance background, she felt intimidated by the stock market, and making individual stock picks. She felt (wrongly, as it turned out) that everyone else in the stock market was smarter than her, and if she started making individual picks, she'd pick incorrectly and consequently lose money.

But, she saw the bigger picture. As she and my dad aged, she realized that millions of others just like her were spending more of their time and money on healthcare. She was also intrigued with technology, and even if she did not know details of computers and high tech, she was astute enough to realize that is where the future was.

Based on her "common person" macro analysis, she broke her money in to a few major sectors:

Healthcare-25%
Technology-25%
Utilities-15%
Bonds-15%
General Market-20%

She bet on a few trends, but at the same time hedged her bets by investing the rest of the money in safer, more stable arenas, such as bonds and utilities.

After she decided on her allocations, she picked up a copy of Money magazine, and found out which mutual funds were the highest performers in each sector. She then filled out applications, sent checks in, and sat back and reviewed the performance a few times per year. This worked well in the long run.

Research is necessary for investment in this tier. First, strategize your vision. Where do you see the world 10, 20 or 50 years from now? What industries will be dominant? For example, will the steel industry make a comeback? Or maybe the future is new materials, such as carbon nanomaterials. You might not get it exactly right; in fact, the future will probably be a lot different from how you envision it-but you don't have to get it all right to come out ahead. Remember, you are still diversifying.

Once you figure out how you want to allocate capital, research the ETFs or mutual funds that specialize in the target areas. This is a lot easier than researching individual stocks, since there aren't as many, and their performances are fairly comparable.

After you selected the ETFs for your portfolio, you still need regular performance reviews, which I'll discuss later. After all, you need to keep pace with general worldwide trends. You do not want to be holding low tech railroad stocks in a world of high tech self-driving cars.

Tier 4 is a great way to speculate in stocks, to diversify, and to do it with a reasonably small time commitment. If my senior citizen mother did this, so can you.

Possible Implementation – Tier 4
Diversified ETF/Mutual Fund Portfolio
ETF Directory - https://etfdb.com/etfs/

General Market –SPY, QQQ, IWM
Technology – XLK, XWEB, ARKK
Healthcare – VHCIX, IYH, XPH
Bonds – AGG, TLT, GOVT
Commodities – GLD, USO, GSG

CHAPTER 11-TIER 5-PICK YOUR OWN STOCKS-SIMPLE VERSION

TIER 5-Pick Your Own Stocks-Simple Version
Potential Returns-Significantly Above average
Risk Profile-Significantly Above average
Time Horizon-Short to Long Term
Time Commitment-Medium

I wish I had known about stocks when I was a kid. Man, I would have been in heaven. Instead of trying to figure out a way to predict football games to better gamble my allowance-a sports columnist at the Cleveland Press newspaper wondered why a 9-year-old was so interested in football statistics (now you know, Mr. Bob August, rest in peace)-I would have been trying to predict stock prices. Then again, considering I only had a little money from "Young Pros," the grass cutting business I started with my cousin Jamie, I probably would not have gotten too far, too fast.

I was thinking about my 9-year-old self recently, since I now have 3 children of my own just over that age. What life lessons should I be teaching them? Stock picking is one of the first topics that popped into my mind.

So, this tier-picking your own stocks-is what I taught my kids to do. You'll see later on in the Case Studies chapter how they did (spoiler alert: pretty good, they beat two different Wall Street benchmarks), but the great thing about this level is you don't have to be a financial genius or a math wizard to implement it. Just by using common sense and good judgment, you can successfully pick your own stocks.

First, I should be clear that I did not invent this stock picking approach. I learned it from legendary investor Peter Lynch, so I refer you to his great book "One Up On Wall Street" for more in-depth analysis. I am only going to give you the condensed version, along with some examples, here.

In this level of the stock picking pyramid, you pick stocks in companies you know something about. And obviously, what you know has to make you feel good enough about their prospects to buy into the company. Once you find a company you like, you then check its stock performance for verification. If you think a company is great, but the stock price is continually dropping, perhaps your view of the company is a bit off. But if the stock price trend agrees with your analysis, perhaps it is a good buy.

This approach then combines simple fundamental analysis (do you like the company, what it provides, the way it is run? Those observations many times mimic good/performance shown in annual report metrics) with simple technical analysis (if the stock price is trending up, most technical measures will agree "buy").

One obvious flaw with this approach is that there are hundreds of companies that the typical consumer/investor will never have experience with. After all, unless you live near a Lubrizol chemical plant, you probably know absolutely nothing about this stock, or this company. They may be a great investment (actually, Warren Buffett's Berkshire Hathaway owns it, so that is a good sign), but since this tier is based on personal experience, you probably would not have it in your potential stock universe.

So, be careful with this approach, because the tendency will be to be concentrated with consumer goods, entertainment companies and companies that are typically in the news. You will overlook many good investments this way.

Note that this approach does not involve developing fundamental or technical stock screeners to whittle down your list. Nor does it involve any in-depth analysis of the company's financials or competitors. You could certainly do both, though. It just involves keeping your eyes open and relying on your judgment to determine the good companies. A few examples are given below.

Disney

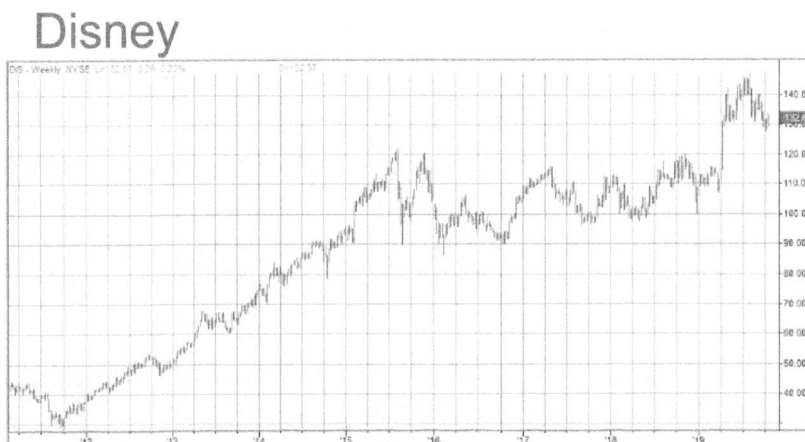

Figure 6- Disney (DIS) Stock, 2011-2019

Growing up, I was never a huge Disney fan. Sure I once went to Disney World as a child, and I saw many of their movies, but I was more of a Bugs Bunny fan than a Mickey Mouse fan. Just personal preference I suppose. That all changed when I had children.

As my kids grew towards kindergarten age, I saw other parents making regular trips to Disney in Florida. I scoffed and told myself that would never be me. Yet, some 12 vacations to Disney later, here I am!

So, I know a lot about Disney through my kids. One thing I always noticed as a hyper vigilant parent was the condition of the theme park restrooms. After all, what parent wants their child touching god knows what in a dirty theme park bathroom? I remember during my first Disney visit since childhood that the restrooms were always exceptionally clean. That stuck in my memory.

Now, you might think "how does a clean bathroom reflect a company's stock performance?" Well, it probably doesn't, at least not directly. It is a small detail in the grand scheme of running a theme park and a huge international corporation. But Walt Disney was all about details. He told his animators "we have to make it better than it has to be." That philosophy obviously still exists at Disney, as I saw in the sparkling bathrooms. They were cleaner than they needed to be. I'm sure many others noticed that, too.

And it wasn't just the bathrooms. It was practically everything in the theme parks and the resort. Workers were friendly and helpful, busses ran on time, rides broke down infrequently, the grounds were meticulously landscaped, and on and on. Just a great overall experience. I concluded that this was a well-run company, worth owning stock in.

Turns out my conclusion was a good indicator of how well the company was run. From my first observation during my 2011 visit, Disney stock has soared. Clean bathrooms weren't the reason, but I think that was a good outward indication of the company's health and prospects. Something that everyone can observe.

Troubling note: During my last visit in late 2018, I noticed a change. Bathrooms not as clean, the parks not as crisp and tidy, the resorts looking a bit more rundown. Possibly just an anomaly- Disney stock is still doing great-but maybe it is a warning sign. After all, if clean bathrooms got me into Disney, shouldn't dirty bathrooms get me out?

AT&T

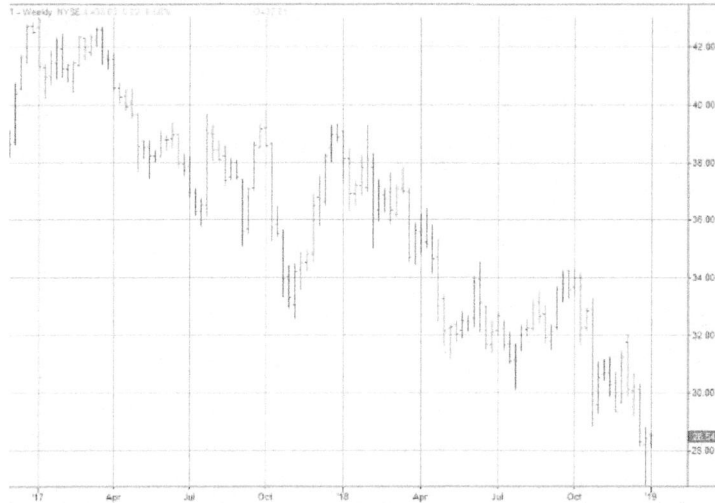

Figure 7- AT&T (T) Stock Price, 2017-2019

Everyone can agree that AT&T has been a large and successful company over many years. But, should you invest in it? Personal experience with AT&T might tell you all you need to know.

Back in late 2016, my family moved a few miles, to a new home in an adjoining suburb outside of Cleveland, Ohio. As part of moving, I had to transfer my phone landline service (I am one of the few people still with a landline, because of a security system). This was supposed to be amazingly simple. Just call AT&T and have them transfer the phone number from our old house to our new house. I imagine it is just a few software commands. Easy stuff.

Unfortunately, not so simple for AT&T! They messed up this elementary phone number transfer about as badly as you can imagine. In fact, probably worse than you can imagine. For example, at one point in the *month long* phone switching saga, I was treated as a "new" customer, and had to get my credit checked. This was even though I had already been an AT&T customer for the previous 15 years, with nary a late payment!

I ended up having about 10 conversations with 10 different AT&T reps, scattered all across the US (and possibly the globe, based on some indecipherable accents I encountered). Lots of wasted resources on AT&T's end, all to perform a very simple task.

Needless to say, I did not even consider buying AT&T stock. My conclusion: AT&T was a terribly run company. That was all I needed to know.

The market thought the same thing. Although the price has recovered in 2019, in 2017 and 2018 the stock was in a near continuous downhill slide.

AT&T is a good example of how observing companies misbehave can be enlightening.

This "see with your eyes" analysis is excellent and does not require any deep investigation. You simply observe what you see and then act on it. This approach helped me sell my McDonald's stock a few years ago (again, the dirty bathroom syndrome), and I regret the times I did not act on it (I've loved going to Costco for years, so why have I never owned their stock?).

As I mentioned earlier, this is the tier I taught my kids. At the time I taught them, they ranged in age from 9 to 13. I sat them down, and instead of explaining book value or earnings per share, I explained they could be owners of a company, and they should be owners of companies they knew and liked.

With that advice, I had them set off to find some stocks. I had no idea what they'd pick exactly, but I was thinking Disney, Costco and a few restaurant chains might be on their list. I forgot, however, that they spend a ton of their time on their computers and electronic devices, watching videos and playing games. So, they selected some companies they liked, such as Apple, Google, Dell, Activision, Nvidia and a few others. Task 1 of the level was completed!

Next, for each of the picks (each child selected his or her own portfolio, but there was definitely overlap), I sat each down and asked them why they picked the stock. I required a logical reason for the company and its prospects, based on their observations. We eliminated some stocks during this step.

Finally, we took a look at the stock price chart. The key is the stock price should reflect their observations. The price should be moving up. In technical terms, the price was likely above major moving averages, and therefore in "buy" territory. I did not check that explicitly, as I did not want to overwhelm my kids with analysis. Maybe someday soon, though…

In almost all cases, the stock passed the price-moving-up "eyeball" requirement. That analysis put it on the "buy" list, so the then bought those stocks. I'll reveal later how their picks have done.

Summing up, Tier 5 not all that difficult. Just pick companies you like and have had a good experience with, and before buying, first verify your favorable observations by examining the price chart. It is a step up in risk from earlier tiers, since you are now picking individual stocks as opposed to a basket of stocks. And, you will spend a lot of time observing companies in action as you go about your day. But, the rewards are potentially higher, if you select good stocks.

Possible Implementation – Tier 5
Pick Your Own Stock Portfolio

Kevin's Favorites – DIS, COST, FB

See Case Study Chapter For Portfolios Listed Below
Portfolio O –ATVI, AMZN, GOOG
Portfolio K – GOOG, AAPL, ATVI, AMZN
Portfolio A – DELL, ATVI, AAPL, GOOG, NVDA

CHAPTER 12-TIER 6-ADDING A MARKET TIMER TO YOUR APPROACH

TIER 6-Adding a Market Timer To Your Approach
Potential Returns-Above average
Risk Profile-Above average
Time Horizon-All
Time Commitment-Medium to Large

Boy, this is weird, I thought to myself as I looked around. All the old guys look like zombies, shuffling along at a snail's pace, with dead eyed straight ahead stares. What did I get myself into?

It was my first day at my first real job out of college, at Rockwell International in El Segundo, California. I thought hi-tech aerospace defense work would be livelier than this. Instead, I felt like I was in a nursing home, surrounded by a bunch of lifeless souls.

"Hey, what's up with all the depressed looking graybeards?" I asked my friend Ken, who I had met during an interview 6 months prior. He had started a few months before I had, so he knew the lay of the land. He had a knack for reading people and situations nearly flawlessly.

"Oh, those guys were supposed to retire last year, but when the stock market crash of October 1987 happened, they lost big in their retirement accounts. They have to keep working now, even though they want to retire. A pretty sad situation."

Pretty sad indeed. But, that is a major investing risk. Sure, the market goes up over time, but it also has occasional and violent drops.

If your timing is unlucky, you might buy right before a crash, or have to sell right after a crash. Years of careful investing (hopefully following one of the previously discussed tiers) can all be wiped away in one market move. Don't forget that.

What can an investor do? One option-no pun intended-is to purchase put options as a form of insurance. Of course, since it is insurance, it will cost you. During a market crash, your long stock portfolio will decrease in value, and put options will increase. Depending how you have it set up, you could offset most of the risk from a crash. In the long run, however, you may find yourself paying a lot more for insurance than it is actually worth.

Another alternative is to try to time your market purchases. This is fairly easy to do, applies to all tiers, and can improve performance. The downside is it requires more time and effort.

The simplest market timer is using the 250 day (1 year) average as a proxy for market health. In this case, you buy your stock or ETF only if the general market is trading above its 250 day average. You then sell when it is below the 250 day average. So, the rule is you are always long the stock, unless general market conditions, as measured by the 250 day average, reflect a bear market.

This is best shown via an example. Let's look at GE stock from 1980 to 2017, at which point General Electric (GE) became a recognizably bad stock to own (based on news reports and the stock price. In this case, both fundamental and technical measures would be screaming "sell!"). Investor A purchases General Electric back in January 1980 and holds on to it for all this time. Investor B uses the market timing trick described above.

The differences in results are quite astounding, as shown by the equity curves for both scenarios. Investor B would have about 25% more profit, and much lower risk (measured by drawdown). In this case, market timing works out very favorably.

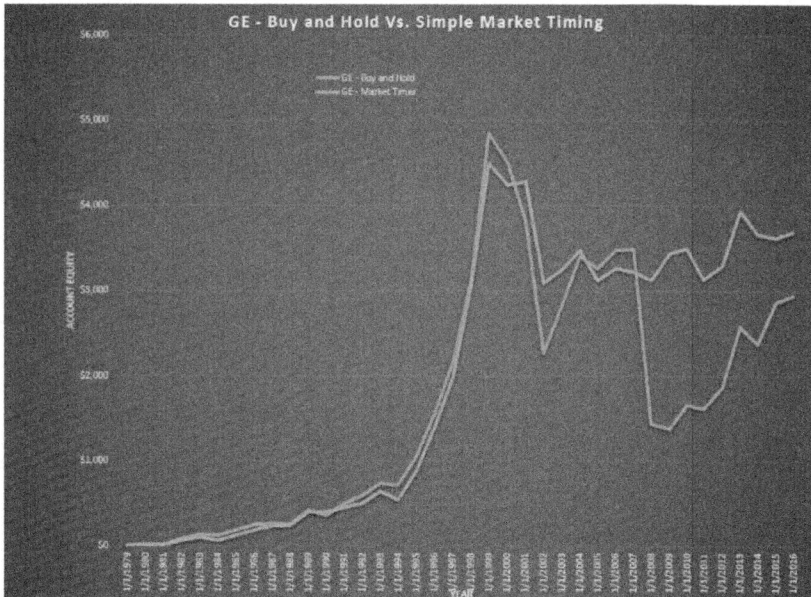

Figure 8- Buy and Hold vs. Market Timing, GE Stock

But, that is not always the case. The reason this approach worked with GE is that GE had its up and downs during the test period, and the market timing switch helped by exiting longs during the down periods. For a stock that continuously performed well during the test period, exiting during market drops won't make sense. In general, the efficacy of market timing is likely related to the stock's beta value. Beta is a measure of how much a stock price changes relative to the overall market. This approach is best with high beta value stocks-stocks that more closely track the overall market average.

Could you improve on that with different timing methods? Very possibly, yes. For example, instead of the 52 week performance of the market being the switch, you could have the stock's performance itself be the switch. Then, when the stock dropped, eventually the long position would be exited. Or you could use a shorter, more responsive average, such as a 3 month or 6 month average.

Another possible timing tool is the Relative Strength Index, developed by Welles Wilder. It is a technical analysis indicator that identifies so-called overbought and oversold areas. With this indicator, you'd buy when the indicator suggested an oversold regime (typically after a rapid drop in stock price), and sell when the indicator reached oversold territory.

<u>Possible Implementation - Tier 6</u>

Market Timers

Be sure to test any timer before implementing

1. Buy only when price is above 250 day moving average, sell belo'
2. Buy only when 14 period RSI in oversold territory (<30), sell >70

Use above timers with stock price, or general index price

More potential timers:

https://seekingalpha.com/article/4079476-10-market-timing-strategies-compared

---

As you can imagine, the possibilities for timing entry and exit start to become endless, especially if you add in fundamental factors (for example, only buy if earnings per share the last X quarters is rising) or technical factors (only buy 52-week highs, sell at 12 week lows). This type of effort becomes its own higher level tier, which I'll discuss next.

CHAPTER 13-TIER 7-BUILD YOUR OWN STOCK PICKER/TRADER ALGO

TIER 7-Build Your Own Stock Picker/Trader Algo
Potential Returns-Above average
Risk Profile-Above Average To Very Large
Time Horizon-All, Usually Short Term
Time Commitment-Large (a part-time job at least!)

Imagine a computer making trades for you, deciding what stocks to buy and sell, never missing a trade, never being emotional about losses or missed gains, just steadily building your portfolio.

Sounds great, doesn't it?

Problem is, it doesn't quite exist. At least it never works as good as it sounds. Trades are missed on occasion, the algorithms (algos) that decide when to buy and sell don't always pick the right trades, and emotion still has a way of creeping into the picture.

Welcome to the world of algo trading, the next tier in the stock trading pyramid.

I am pretty familiar with algo trading, having done it on a part time and full time basis in the futures and forex markets for a number of years. I can tell you firsthand it can be extremely rewarding, but also extremely difficult. It can take up your time, without producing any favorable results. It is DEFINITELY not for everyone.

Here is a short little description of algo trading, taken from my book "Intro to Algo Trading."

Algo trading is all about rules. In fact, it is nothing but rules. No discretion. No human judgment.

Trading algorithms can be as simple as you want, or as complicated as you want.

How simple? Here is a basic 2 line strategy:

If close < average close of last 5 bars, go long
If close > average close of last 5 bars, go short

Over the past 15 years, this strategy made money with some stocks, yet lost money with others. Algo trading involves a lot of testing-seeing what works for what stocks, and in what situations.

That was a very simple algo. In contrast, some algorithmic strategies are extremely complicated, too. There are traders with single algorithms that run 25,000 lines of code or more-real rocket science stuff!

There are two keys to trading algorithms:

1. They can be tested. Most algorithms can be historically tested, commonly referred to as a backtest. This turns out to be a major advantage of creating algorithms. For algos that cannot be historically tested, they almost always can be live tested in simulation mode, with proper precautions and some caveats. In either case, the trader can usually determine the acceptability of the strategy BEFORE trading it with real money.

2. Algorithms are rigidly defined. If the algorithm sees a long setup today, it will tell you to go long. If it sees that same setup tomorrow, it will tell you to go long again. The algo only follows its programmed rules. It doesn't care what the Fed thinks, does not care about the news, and does not care that Jim Cramer screamed that a certain stock was a

buy last night-unless, of course, you program those types of rules into your algorithm. The algo is consistent in how it follows the rules.

Many traders speak of "black boxes," a special type of algorithm. With black boxes, the rules (the algorithm) remain hidden to the trader. He or she only gets the entry and exit signals and has no idea how those signals were produced.

That type of algorithm might sound unappealing or scary, but many people like that approach. It is really hard to interfere with computer code you cannot even see!

Some Examples Of Algo Trading

- A retail trader, trading at home. He works full time, so trading is his hobby. Every night, he downloads the latest prices, calculates his signals either by hand or on a computer, and places trades according to the rules. He may or may not check positions during the day, but since he places orders during non-work hours, he knows he is following his strategies each and every day.

- A prop trader, trading full time. He enters and exits trades all day long, again according to set rules. He never, ever deviates from the rules, since he knows his boss spot checks his trades for adherence to the rules.

- A hedge fund computer code, written by numerous PhDs in math, statistics and physics. The computer code they run has 50,000 lines of code, and does everything–enter trades, exits trades, calculates position sizing, automatically performs rollovers, etc. A junior trader is always nearby, monitoring trades in case of a malfunction, but the computer controls the show. The strategies they run can be on the order of microseconds (in and out quickly), day trades of a few hours, or swing trades lasting weeks.

- A professional retail trader, using a standard retail platform such as Tradestation. He creates strategies, then lets Tradestation run those strategies automated. The trader is closely monitoring positions, because as Tradestation personnel say "automated trading does not mean unattended trading." He can trade quite a few automated strategies, assuming he has enough capital, and if his strategies are diversified enough.

What makes these people algorithmic traders is that they follow strict rules for entry and exit. That is the real key–they are 100% rule followers. With those strict rules, they can historically backtest their approaches, and while "past performance is not indicative of future results" (as a U.S. government disclaimer correctly states), it is very nice to realize that the strategies traded have worked in the past.

So, algo trading is definitely something the dedicated stock investor can try. But, if you decide to try it, prepare for a LOT of work. It is not easy finding "edges"-ways to profit from market inefficiencies-and properly testing them is pretty difficult, too.

But, if this sounds like a worthwhile challenge for you, I suggest you read the following books for more information:

"Introduction To Algo Trading: How Retail Traders Can Successfully Compete With Professional Traders,"–by Kevin Davey

"Algorithmic Trading: Winning Strategies and Their Rationale,"-By Dr. Ernest Chan

"Building Winning Algorithmic Trading Systems, + Website: A Trader's Journey From Data Mining to Monte Carlo Simulation to Live Trading,"-by Kevin Davey

Some Example Stock and ETF Algos

Here are some simple algos I have used on stocks and ETFs. These algos are strictly technical indicator based algos. You could also create algos that incorporated fundamental factors.

You can get the code for these algos in Tradestation and NinjaTrader format by signing up for the book bonuses (details at beginning and end of this book).

Strategy 1-BreakOut

Entry:

Buy if the close is the highest close of the last X bars, and if the close is less than the previous close plus 1.5 times the recent Average True Range (a good measurement of volatility).

This can have a Sell Short if the exact opposite occurs, but for this example I have turned it off.

Exit:

Sell if the loss becomes greater than Y dollars, or if Z bars have passed since the trade was entered.

Here is how that strategy looks when applied to AAPL stock.

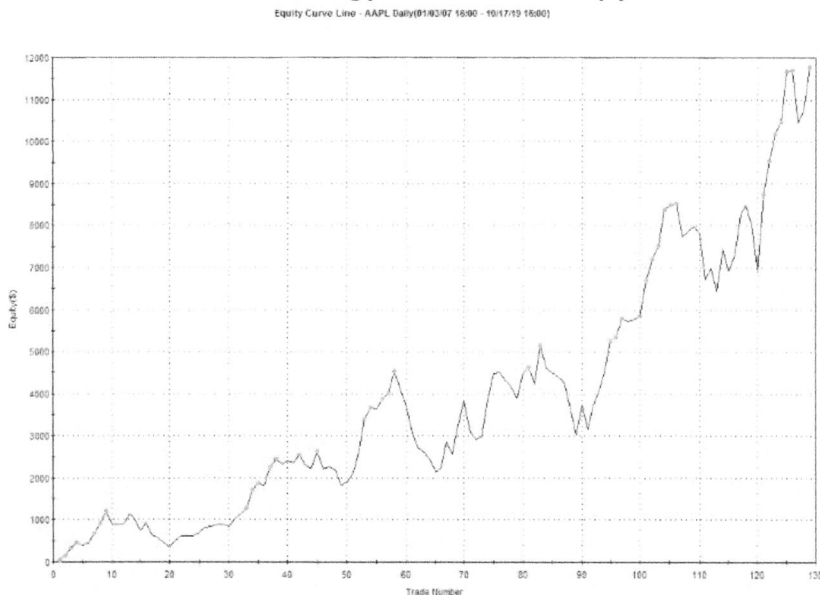

Figure 9- Algo Strategy 1 With AAPL Stock

Strategy 2-Open/Close Gapper

Entry:

Define medium gap days and large gap days (open today compared to previous close), based on the Average True Range. On medium gap days sell short if the gap is down and buy if the gap is up. On large gap days buy if the gap is down and sell short if the gap is up.

Note that this strategy is a bit unique, since the gaps are calculated as open to previous close, not open to previous high or low. Testing showed using previous close was a better idea.

Exit:

Exit if a stop loss or profit target is hit.

Here is how that strategy looks when applied to GOOG stock.

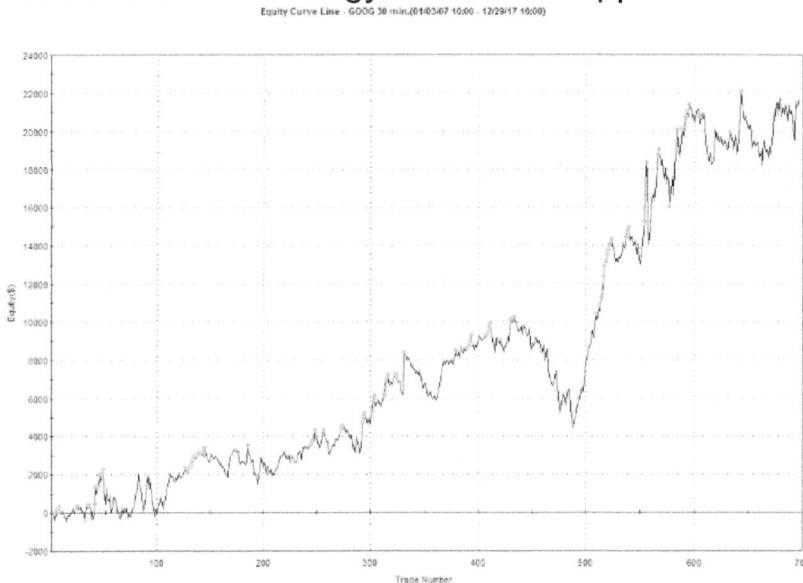

Equity Curve Line - GOOG 30 min.(01/03/07 10:00 - 12/29/17 16:00)

Figure 10- Algo Strategy 2 With GOOG Stock

Strategy 3-Break Stop

Entry:

If the current position is flat, buy the next bar at the current close plus a factor multiplied by the recent lookback period range. Sell short the next bar at the current close minus a factor multiplied by the recent lookback period range.

Exit:

Exit long or short at a profit (limit order) or loss (stop order) based on the highest high or lowest low of the lookback length.

Here is how that strategy looks when applied to the SPY ETF.

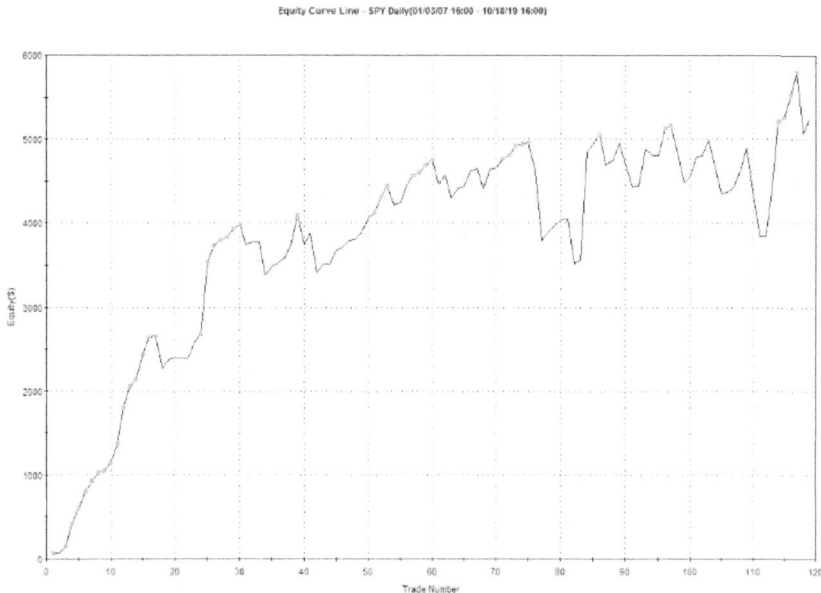

Figure 11- Algo Strategy 3 With SPY ETF

Note these example algos just touch the surface of what you can create. You might also notice that the performance of each is good, but not great. In fact, I'll wager that with a quick Internet search, you will find MUCH better looking equity curves. Just remember that most algo equity curves you see are highly optimized. Those types of strategies tend not to do well in real time. The ones I show above are not highly optimized, hence they look worse. But they likely will perform better in real time.

The key with building algo trading strategies is not in the idea (although most ideas turn out to be garbage), but rather in the process used to backtest and verify the strategy. Achieving a good match beyond historical and real time results is the goal, not just having a nice looking backtest.

If you decide to pursue algo trading, prepare for a lot of blood, sweat and tears. It is hard work.

Possible Implementation - Tier 7
Algo Strategies

Be sure to test any strategy before implementing

1,2,3. 3 strategies given above

4. Buy if close > close X bars ago, sell if opposite (simple momentum)

5. Buy 52-week highs, sell 52-week lows

6. Add earnings or earnings per share to each (buy only if earnings trend is up)

7. Add a filter for stocks trading at less than book value

CHAPTER 14-TIER 8-EXOTIC APPROACHES-OPTIONS, SHORTING STOCK, AND MORE

TIER 8-Exotic Approaches-Options, Shorting Stock and More
Potential Returns-Extreme
Risk Profile-Extreme
Time Horizon-Typically Short Term
Time Commitment-Large

For those of you looking for extreme returns in the stock markets, but with a possibly "lose it all" downside risk, here are a few avenues you could pursue.

Options

For traders willing to take risks, or those without a lot of trading capital, stock options offer an alternative. With options, you don't actually own the stock, you own the *right* to buy or sell the stock.

These rights are much cheaper than owning the stock outright, and therefore if the underlying stock increases in value, your options could skyrocket in price, providing you with an excellent rate of return.

On the flip side, most options actually expire worthless, in part since they have a limited life. If you buy a call option, and the stock price stays flat or goes down before expiration, then your option becomes worthless. Studies have shown that up to 80% of stock options expire with no value.

Options are a mathematician's dream, with a whole alphabet of Greek letters is used to describe various aspects of them. Heck, a Nobel Prize was once awarded to 2 developers of the Black-Scholes model-a complicated but fairly accurate option pricing technique.

If you are thinking about options, prepare for a lot of math, a lot of studying, frequent losses with expired options and a few big winners, which hopefully make you profitable overall.

Obviously, in this book I don't have the space to give option buying (and selling, which is a whole other world) a fair treatment, so instead I refer you to a couple of good books on the subject:

"Options as a Strategic Investment: Fifth Edition,"-by Lawrence McMillian

"The Options Playbook: Featuring 40 strategies for bulls, bears, rookies, all-stars and everyone in between,"-by Brian Overby

Shorting Stock

Up until this point, I've discussed only buying stock. When the stock price goes up, you make money. When it goes down, you lose money.

Buy, did you know you can turn this upside down, and actually make money when the stock goes down, and lose money when the stock goes up?

This approach is called "shorting" stock, and since stock prices can only go to zero on the downside, but theoretically can go to infinity on the upside, it is a limited reward and unlimited risk situation.

If you buy a stock and go on a 2 year around the world cruise, you could make money if the stock goes up, but you'll never lose more than your initial investment.

On the other hand, if you short sell a stock and go on a 2 year around the world cruise, you could make money if the stock goes down or goes bankrupt, but you could lose an unlimited amount of money if the stock skyrockets.

Short selling stock is not for the faint of heart.

If this sounds confusing, just remember the phrase "buy low and sell high." That is what everyone wants to do. It is just the order that may be reversed:

Typical stock investors buy low first and sell high later.
Those shorting stock instead sell high first and buy low later.

Again, with this book I can't do short selling justice, but here is a classic book that will get you on your way:

"How to Make Money Selling Stocks Short"-by William J. O'Neill and Gil Morales

Other Approaches

There are many other ways to turning stock investing into a high reward, but potentially high risk, endeavor. I don't necessarily recommend these approaches for most investors, as they are mainly best left to experts.

Trading On Margin-When you trade on margin, you do not need to have funds for the whole purchase amount of your stock. Instead, you broker loans you a good portion of the amount, at a fairly reasonable interest rate. If the stock performs-if the return on the stock is greater than the loan interest rate you are paying-you effectively make money with the broker's money. On the downside, if the stock underperforms, you'll pay the margin loan, and have only losses to show for it.

Brokers love clients who trade on margin, so that alone should make you extremely wary of doing it! This is appropriate only for the serious, experienced investor.

Takeover Candidates-Some stock pickers like to guess at which companies might be bought out by other companies. If and when this happens, the stock price can shoot up, and the investor makes a windfall profit. But, as you can imagine, this is infrequent, and proposed deals fall apart constantly. It is almost like chasing ghosts-you may never catch a profitable trade this way.

Near Bankrupt Companies-If you like getting a good deal, buying bankrupt companies, or near bankrupt companies, may be for you. The stock market can undervalue shares of these companies, so those that invest in them could see nice returns. Sometimes bankrupt companies are bailed out, sometimes they sell their assets for much more than expected, and sometimes they even recover and later thrive. But more times than not, these stocks eventually go to zero, wiping out all investors.

If you are thinking of this type of investing, prepare to stare at financial reports and legal documents for a long time, before you pick the right "sinking ship" company to invest in.

Penny Stocks-"Watch out!!!" is the phrase that best describes penny stocks. Sure, you can buy a stock for 2 cents a share, and if it only rises 2 more cents a share, you've doubled your money. Doesn't that sound easy? After all, it is only 2 cents.

The problem: the stock costs 2 cents for a reason, and it usually is not a good reason. Suspect companies, sometimes operated by shady characters, with even shadier brokers, is the land you'll be living in with penny stocks.

Remember how I cautioned you on newsletters earlier? Well, there are quite a few that tout penny stocks. Here is the typical ploy of the unscrupulous ones:

1. The penny stock operator finds a low price, low trading volume stock to exploit. Sometimes it is actually the company itself behind the exploitation.

2. The insiders-the newsletter publisher, possibly company officials, friends and family-slowly and secretly buy the stock, trying not to raise the price.   Let's say they buy over a few weeks at 5 cents a share. They spread out their buying to keep daily volume low and not raise any suspicions.

3. Great news is published by the company, or the penny stock is rated a "strong buy" by the newsletter.

4. Hundreds or thousands of "sheep" investors jump into the stock; raising the price while creating a lot of buzz and high volume.

5. The "sheep" are the newsletter subscribers and anyone unfortunate to hear the sales pitch. They buy, but guess who is selling? The insiders, that's who. As the price goes up, they sell all their shares to the sheep. Now the sheep own the stock at 15 cents, the insiders have sold all their shares at 10 to 15 cents-a 100-200% return-and life goes on.

6. Now comes the "sheep shearing." News fades away, people lose interest, and the stock returns to it pre-hype level of 5 cents (or worse). The sheep lose money.

Of course, this is not always true-some penny stocks legitimately succeed. If you invest in penny stocks, look for and avoid the above scenario. Don't be a sheep!

Possible Implementation - Tier 8

Option Strategies
Buy at the money call options
Buy LEAP (long term) options
Sell covered calls

Other Strategies
Avoid (or be EXTREMELY careful with):
Penny Stocks
Trading On Margin
Buying Near Bankrupt Companies

CHAPTER 15-PROTECTING YOUR INVESTMENT

Most of this book, and really any other stock picking advice you are liable to get, focuses on entering trades. After all, people do refer to it as "stock picking" and "stock recommendations."

Smart traders realize, however, that the entry is only one piece of the puzzle. Knowing when to exit can be as important, financially and emotionally, as the entry itself. There is nothing more deflating than watching a previously profitable stock pick descend into losing territory, all because you did not exit at a better time. Bad timing will hurt you financially and psychologically.

Here are some sensible exit ideas that won't drain your pocketbook.

Exit 1-Initial Stop

Even for long term trades, you will want to protect yourself in case of a crash or downturn. So, before you buy, determine at what point you'd conclude owning this stock was a bad decision.

For example, if you buy the stock at $100, when would you feel you made a bad pick? Maybe the stock needs to fall all the way to $20, or you decide a drop to $90 is far enough.

The right answer involves staying out of the price noise level. If the stock normally moves $1-2 per day, then having a stop at $99 is likely a guaranteed way to exit with a loss. Set your price to have your stop trigger only after a significant decline.

The best stock stop loss point could be determined through backtesting, if you are so inclined, or it could just be something you feel comfortable with. The key is to have this exit point in mind, hopefully written down, and ideally placed as a good-till-canceled order in the market.

Example: You buy a stock at $100.   In reviewing the price chart, you see that it almost never has gone below $80 in the past 3 years. And since a drop to $80 would be a 20% decrease (which is the max you feel comfortable with), you place a good-til-cancelled order to exit at $80 on a stop. Place the order immediately after purchasing the stock. Hopefully this will never be hit, but if it is, you stand to lose about 20% of your initial investment (due to stop loss slippage, you could lose more than that).

Exit 2-Trailing Stop

In addition to an initial stop, you might want to trail a stop as the stock price rises. Let's say that as the stock rises, you always want to "lock in" at least $10 profit per share (you could use percentages, too). As the price rose, you would regularly update your stop loss price to be $10 below the most recent high or high close. BUT, the stop would never go down; it would only move up.

Example: You buy a stock at $100, the price is now $120. You enter a stop order to sell at $110. If the price falls to $115, the stop is still at $110. If the price hits $110 you exit.

Now let's say the price increase to $140.   You new stop order will be to exit on a drop to $130. And as the price continues to fluctuate, you move the stop up if the price goes up, but if the stock goes down, you never move it below $130.

This trailing technique is a pretty neat way to protect your profits, but it is not without risk. If the trailing stop is too close to the price, you will likely get stopped out, and if then the price recovers and reaches a new high, it will be without you owning it any longer!

All things considered, this trailing stop is a great way to prevent winners from turning into losers, and psychologically feels pretty good ("hey, at least I got out with a profit."). But, for long term traders, it can be detrimental, as the stop will trigger before the uptrend is over.

Exit 3-Breakeven Stop

As I mentioned before, watching winners turn into losers is just awful. It really destroys your psyche and obviously hits your wallet, too. One solution to this is a breakeven stop. For the $100 per share stock purchase, once the stock reaches $110, you decide you want out if the price falls back to $100. In other words, you want to at least breakeven on the stock purchase.

This can be emotionally satisfying-it is neat knowing that come-what-may, you likely will not lose money on this stock-but it does have a potential downside. Just as with trailing stops, there will be times where the stock drops to your breakeven point, taking you out of the trade, before reversing and continuing its upward climb. What is worse: breakeven on a stock before it goes lower, or watching one of your picks reach new highs without you owning it?

Only you can decide if a breakeven stop is appropriate for you. The longer term your perspective, the less likely you need this sort of protection.

Exit 4-High Point Exit

Up until now, I have discussed exiting only as the price falls. Well, why can't you exit as the price rises? You definitely can, and that is the idea between a high point, or target, exit.

Here is how this would work. You buy a stock at $100 per share, and decide if it ever hits $150, you want to cash out and exit with a nice 50% profit. Sounds great, right? After all, who doesn't enjoy a 50% profit?

The drawback to this type of exit is regret. When you exit with a profit, you are happy, but if the stock continues its upward journey, that happiness will soon turn to depression. You picked right, but can no longer benefit (unless you get back in at a higher price).

If you are a short-term or frequent trader, this might be a good exit to use. For longer term investors, though, this type of exit will only serve to limit profits from good stock selections.

Example: Buy a stock at $100. Place a good till canceled order to exit at $150 on a limit order.

Exit 5-No Exit At All

The most daring among us have no stop, except at $0. This type of non-exit prevents you from getting stopped out by random market noise. But, if the investment goes to $0, you are effectively out of the game-you'd have to buy your next stock with new money.

99% of traders and investors should avoid this exit.

CHAPTER 16-
DIVERSIFICATION, PORTFOLIO
MANAGEMENT AND POSITION
SIZING

Now that I've described the various levels of stock investing, from simple buying of a SPY ETF to picking your own stocks to creating an algo trading system to employing risky, esoteric investment techniques, it is time to talk about how to put it all together:

Should you just buy one stock?
Do you need a diversified portfolio?
How many shares should you buy?

These questions are answered in this chapter.

Imagine that you can buy 1 stock for the rest of your life. You get to pick which one, but you have to put all your money into it, and you have to either keep it forever, or keep your money in cash instead.

Laughable, right?

Hopefully so. If you think that picking only 1 stock is a crazy idea, then intuitively you already understand diversification, portfolio building and position sizing.

Just to be clear, here is how I define these terms:

Diversification-being in a wide variety of stocks and investments. This could include different market sectors (Financials, consumer goods), different categories of stocks (growth stocks, value stocks, dividend stocks) and even timeframes (short-term holdings, long-term investments).

Portfolio Building-How exactly you implement this diversification approach-what you own, how the portfolio is allocated amongst different sectors and styles.

Position Sizing-Two traders can both own Facebook, IBM and Costco stock, yet have wildly different results, depending on how they size their positions. Position size is simply the amount of a stock you have, and can be thought of in terms of dollar amount (you own $2500 of Costco) or as a percentage of your portfolio (Costco stock represents 10.6% of your portfolio).

Diversification is key to achieving a successful stock investing career.   In 1990, Harry Markowitz won a Nobel Prize for his work with diversification. In 1952, he created the Markowitz Portfolio-one where diversification lowered the portfolio's risk for any given return.

Further studies have confirmed and expounded on Markowitz's theory. Currently, the consensus is that 10-20 stocks, in a variety of industries, with a variety of styles, is a good balance between having enough diversification, yet not being overly complicated. A portfolio of 500 stocks might be nice for diversification, but you do not necessarily need that many to reap the benefits.

Obviously, one way to be diversified, with little or no effort, is to buy an index, following the Tier 1 plan. Putting all your money in SPY provides diversification, and you would not even have to worry about position sizing. The relative position size of each stock in the index is pre-determined, so you don't have to do it.

If you are at a higher tier on the stock pyramid, for example at step 5-picking your own stocks-you will want to be careful to avoid concentration in any one area. As I'll show in the case study chapter, my children have picked mainly growth stocks in computers and technology. I need to help them reduce that concentration. They don't know-but I know-that they also have some college fund SPY type investments, so they do have diversification.

Let's assume you build your portfolio as shown:

Consumer goods-20%
Technology-40%
Heavy Industry-20%
Financials-20%

With the following distribution:

Value stocks-20%
Growth stocks-50%
Dividend stocks 30%

Even once you have this general outline, within each area you may have multiple stocks, and you will have to decide on position sizing. For example, let's say for consumer goods you decide on Costco, Wal-Mart and Target. Should you just allocate 33% to each, or possibly some other weighting that favors one of the group?

As you can see, building a portfolio of diversified stocks can become very complicated. Plus, there is no correct answer. Sure, historical review will reveal an optimum portfolio structure, but the best portfolio for the last 10 years will not be the best portfolio for the next 10. And portfolio allocation has a huge impact of your overall results.

My advice? First, you definitely want to create a diversified portfolio of stocks, or at least use index funds to accomplish this. Second, give different sectors equal weighting to start with. Then, as you get comfortable with the ups and downs of your portfolio, you can rebalance during your regular reviews. Do what feels comfortable to you, knowing that history will show that no matter what you do, there would have been a better way-don't let that bother you.

The key with a diversified portfolio is simply having one. Don't put all your eggs in one basket. Don't buy just a single stock and hope for the best.

CHAPTER 17-NEXT STEPS-REGULARLY REVIEW YOUR INVESTMENT PORTFOLIO

Do you own any of these stocks?

Baltimore Opera Hat Company
Trans-Atlantic Zeppelin
Amalgamated Spats
Congreve's Inflammable Powders
U.S. Hay

Chances are no, because 1) they are fictional stocks owned by Montgomery Burns of "The Simpsons" cartoon show, and 2) they are no longer in business, even fictionally.

In an episode of the Simpsons, after decades of disregard the elderly Burns decided to review his stock portfolio. He held the stocks above; companies long since gone. When's the last time a zeppelin flew? Does anyone even wear spats anymore?

Due to neglect, his portfolio was worthless! Don't let that happen to you.

Part of being a responsible stock investor is to have regular reviews of your portfolio. You can do this every 6 months or every year, whatever feels good to you. But DON'T review daily or hourly (some people do!).

You'll drive yourself crazy if you constantly check your portfolio, since stocks regularly go up and down in price. A regular portfolio review every 6-12 months allows for objective analysis.

Maybe that fantastic stock you were confident would soar has instead languished. It might be time to replace it with something else.

Or perhaps that industry specific ETF is now subject to government intervention. For example, what if the government takes over healthcare? That might impact your feelings about healthcare ETFs. You might decide to jettison that ETF.

Regardless of your investment level on the pyramid, you'll want to have regular reviews of both your portfolio, and even your whole approach. I would recommend answering these questions every 6 to 12 months:

* For each stock and ETF in your portfolio: Do I still want to own it?
* Do I want to add any stocks or ETFs to my holdings?
* Do I have any extra money I want to invest, or if so, where should I invest it?
* Do I want to rebalance my portfolio? Possibly keep the same holdings, but just alter the percentages of each one?
* Are there new trends or industries I want to invest in?
* Do I want to stay on the same investment level, or do I want to explore a different level? Is the tier I employ too time consuming? Do I want a move down to free up time? Or, what if I want to spend more time investing? What should I do?

By asking and truthfully answering these questions on a regular basis, you won't get caught like Mr. Burns did, holding a worthless portfolio.

CHAPTER 18-CASE STUDIES

Now that you have seen the various tiers or levels of my stock picking pyramid approach, it is instructive to see how a few of the tiers performed over a short test (just under 7 months). Here are the details:

Contestants:

Tier 1: Invest $10,000 by purchasing the SPY ETF or technology benchmark ETF (QQQ). Hold for the whole test time.

Tier 3: Follow the Legend Warren Buffett. Invest $2500 in four (4) of Warren's recent holdings.

Tier 4: Create a small ETF portfolio. Even though my mom no longer invests, I'll use her allocations from when she was an active investor to allocate $10,000.

Tier 5: Pick your own stocks. I had each of my kids invest $10,000 however they chose. Could they beat the market?

Tier 7: Algo trading strategies. How did the three fairly simple algos I created fare, when each was given $3,333 to trade?

Time Period:

Initiate trading on March 14, 2019. For algos that may have been in a trade before that date, simply enter the position on March 14.

Exit all positions on the close of October 11, 2019.

Caveats:

This is only a 7 month test, and random luck can hurt or help any of the approaches. Don't assume the best performers will remain on top.

This exercise's intent is to show real world implementation of the stock picking pyramid concept.

For this study, as mentioned I'll assume a $10,000 investment, and I'll ignore trading costs for all but tier 5 (I hate ignoring costs, but since many of these cases are buy and hold, trading costs are minimal).

FULL DISCLOSURE: Treat all these results as hypothetical. For Tier 5 (individual stocks selected by my children), the results are based on actual trades, but for all the other tiers, the results are based on simulated trades.

A chart showing final results is shown after the descriptions.

Results:

Tier 1

Invest $10,000 in either SPY or QQQ ETFs. These are generally considered general market or technology benchmarks to beat, so if any of the other tiers beat these results, they will have "beaten Wall Street."

1a. Buy $10,000 SPY (S&P 500 ETF)-buy on March 14, 2019, sell on Oct 11, 2019 >> Gain $626

1b. Alternatively, buy $10,000 QQQ (technology ETF)-buy on March 14, 2019, sell on Oct 11, 2019 >> Gain $831

Tier 3

We are going to follow Warren Buffett, and select 4 of the stocks in his portfolio, selected at random:

$2500 (25%) Apple stock, AAPL -buy on March 14, 2019, sell on Oct 11, 2019 >> Gain $762

$2500 (25%) Bank Of America, BAC -buy on March 14, 2019, sell on Oct 11, 2019 >> Gain $161

$2500 (25%) Delta Airlines stock, DAL -buy on March 14, 2019, sell on Oct 11, 2019 >> Gain $159

$2500 (25%) Wells Fargo Stock, WFC -buy on March 14, 2019, sell on Oct 11, 2019 >> Gain $27

Overall, this subset of Buffett's portfolio gained $1,109 during the test period.

Tier 4

We are going to follow the allocation my mom used in her retirement, buying ETFs and mutual funds:

$2500 (25%) Vanguard Healthcare mutual fund, VGHCX -buy on March 14, 2019, sell on Oct 11, 2019 >> Loss $148

$2500 (25%) Tech Index ETF, QQQ -buy on March 14, 2019, sell on Oct 11, 2019 >> Gain $208

$1500 (15%) Vanguard Utility ETF, VPU -buy on March 14, 2019, sell on Oct 11, 2019 >> Gain $146

$1500 (15%) Short-Term Bond ETF, SHY -buy on March 14, 2019, sell on Oct 11, 2019 >> Gain $19

$2000 (20%) General Market ETF, SPY -buy on March 14, 2019, sell on Oct 11, 2019 >> Gain $125

Overall, this ETF and mutual fund portfolio gained $350 during the test period.

Tier 5

For the stock picking tier, I am going to show 3 portfolios, based on my kids' stock selections. To protect their privacy, I will refer to them as Portfolio O, Portfolio K and Portfolio A, for Owen, Kathryn and Andrew. ☺

Since their picks are from real accounts, the actual amounts they invested varied from $10,000 to just over $11,000. To compare these results to the other tiers, where I hypothetically invested exactly $10,000, I have scaled these results so that $10,000 was the amount invested. That allows an apples to apples comparison with other tiers.

Portfolio O

My oldest put roughly half his money in Amazon (I guess he likes ordering things from Amazon, although I am usually the one paying!), and the remainder split between Google and Activision stock. All technology companies, so definitely more concentrated than desired.

$4816 (48%) Amazon, AMZN -buy on March 14, 2019, sell on Oct 11, 2019 >> Gain $116

$2328 (23%) Google, GOOG -buy on March 20, 2019, sell on Oct 11, 2019 >> Loss $20

$2856 (29%) Activision, ATVI -buy on March 14, 2019, sell on Oct 11, 2019 >> Gain $735

Overall, Portfolio O gained $831 during the test period.

Portfolio A

My youngest bought the most stocks, five, although he allocated 36% to Apple, and more or less divided by rest amongst 4 other tech stocks. Again, too concentrated in one industry, but this is something I'll discuss with him during our regular portfolio review.

$3593 (36%) Apple, AAPL -buy on March 14, 2019, sell on Oct 11, 2019 >> Gain $1054

$1324 (13%) Dell, DELL -buy on March 14, 2019, sell on Oct 11, 2019 >> Loss $164

$1339 (13%) Activision, ATVI -buy on March 20, 2019, sell on Oct 11, 2019 >> Gain $230

$2178 (22%) Google, GOOG -buy on March 20, 2019, sell on Oct 11, 2019 >> Loss $22

$1566 (16%) Nvidia, NVDA-buy on March 20, 2019, sell on Oct 11, 2019 >> Gain $88

Overall, Portfolio A gained $1185 during the test period.

Portfolio K

My daughter, much like her brothers, is into technology. Considering the amount of time she spends on her iPhone, she should be a stockholder just in Apple! Again, she is too technology concentrated.

$1662 (17%) Amazon, AMZN -buy on March 20, 2019, sell on Oct 11, 2019 >> Loss $64

$3310 (33%) Google, GOOG -buy on March 14, 2019, sell on Oct 11, 2019 >> Gain $54

$3659 (37%) Apple, AAPL -buy on March 20, 2019, sell on Oct 11, 2019 >> Gain $917

$1369 (14%) Activision, ATVI -buy on March 14, 2019, sell on Oct 11, 2019 >> Gain $350

Overall, Portfolio K gained $1257 during the test period.

Tier 7

For tier 7, I ran 3 different algo models I developed in early 2019, and created a portfolio with Google, Apple and SPY. Note these results were optimized on data prior to 2019, which is NOT what you usually see when someone shows you algo strategy results. Most results out there are in-sample optimized results. These results are out-of-sample results. These results include slippage and commission costs, because of the amount of trades taken.

$3333 (33%) Google, GOOG -long and short active trader, 42 trades from Mar-Oct 2019   >> Gain $38

$3333 (33%) Apple, AAPL -long active trader, 7 trades from Mar-Oct 2019 >> Gain $385

$3333 (33%) Benchmark ETF, SPY -5 short trades from Mar-Oct 2019 >> Gain $5

Overall, the Tier 7 gained $428 during the test period.

Comparison of Results

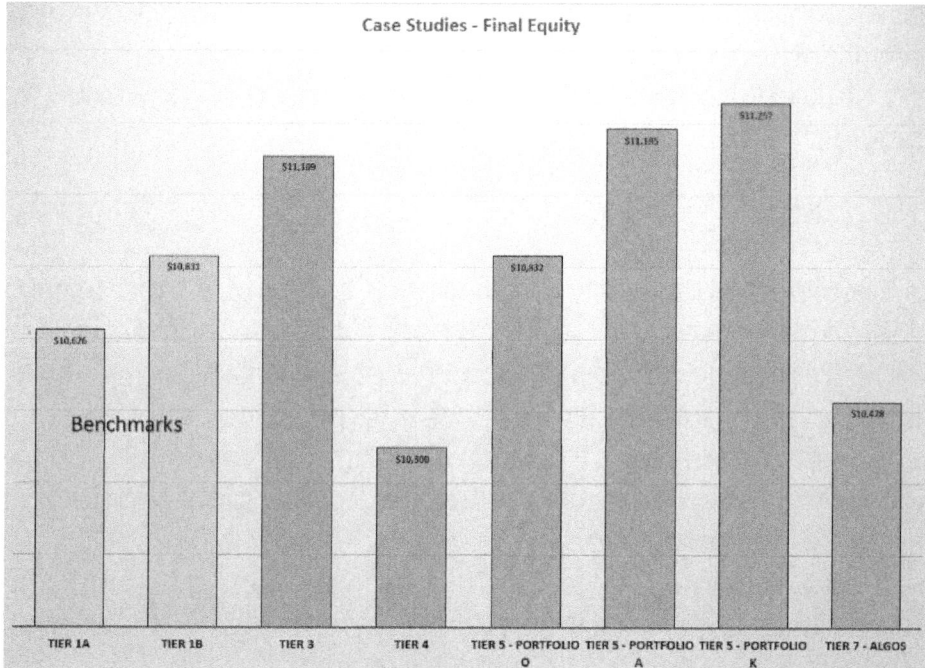

Figure 12- Case Studies - Comparison of Tier Performance

During the test period, all the tiers ended up in positive territory. Overall, girls rule, since my daughter had the best performance with Portfolio K. Note that all of my kids beat the Wall Street benchmark during this test, hence the subtitle of the book. But, investing is not a sprint, it is a marathon. I'll be much more impressed if they continue to beat the benchmark for years or even decades. It isn't easy, but it is possible.

The interesting thing to note is that you can see all the tiers studied produced profits. Depending on how you set it up, your results can be dramatically different for each tier, and some tiers could easily lose money.

One important point I did not discuss here was the amount of drawdown each of the tiers experienced during the test period. Drawdown is an important consideration for any stock portfolio. As in baseball, when you swing for the fences and home runs, you're liable to strike out a lot too. I did not measure drawdown for these case studies.

2021 Update

As I showed earlier, my 3 children (O, A and K) did pretty well from March to November 2019, when I did the comparison test. How have they done since that point? Let's find out!

First, there is nothing like success to produce enthusiasm. And after their performance in the first 7 months of investing, boy were my kids enthused! They all wanted to invest more, to pick more stocks and to do more research.

I encouraged them to save their money from gifts and chores, and maybe invest it in more stocks if they wanted to. Only one took advantage of that, adding $1,000 to his account.

Part of being a good long term investor is actually adding money to the account. A good rule of thumb – one that I am teaching to my kids – is to save 10% of your income for savings. That is a great way to build a stock account. It might not seem like much now, but in 30-40 years you will thank me for that advice.

From November 2019 to the time of this writing (March 2021) all three of my kids held regular portfolio reviews every few months. Based on the reviews, they either stayed with the stocks they had originally picked, or made some changes, switching out stocks in their respective portfolios. My role was to make sure they had solid reasons for their decisions; in other words, I was instilling good investing skills.

The end decisions to buy and sell were still theirs and theirs alone. This is an important trading and investing habit: take responsibility for your trading decisions. If you don't, it becomes easy to blame your failures on a guru's bad advice. My philosophy is since you own the money, you need to own the decisions too!

From the initial review in November 2019 until March 2021, two major events happened during this time period. Both turned out to be great instructional situations.

First, in early 2020, the Covid-19 crisis shook all investors to the core. Who knew how far the market was going to fall in March 2020, when the world seemed to be coming to an end? Panic seemed everywhere!

Of course, my children investors were not immune to this. So in March, when things looked bleakest, we did an "emergency" portfolio review. Should we just go to all cash? Should we sell current holdings and buy other stocks? Should we just stay pat, and do nothing?

After this review, all three of them decided to just keep their holdings. They felt all their stocks were long term plays, and that there was no need to panic. Turned out to be a great move!

The second major event was the GameStop fiasco of early 2021. I discuss that more fully in another chapter, but luckily for me my kids were not taken in by the get rich quick hype surrounding GameStop and a few other stocks. Since they had no money to invest (they were 100% invested already), they decided to just keep their current holdings, and not sell any holdings to buy GameStop. Wise choice!

The stock market always seems to be teaching lessons, and 2020 and 2021 were no exception. Stay true to your core investing principles, and things will likely turn out OK.

So, after 2 years of investing in the stock market, using the pyramid blueprint I describe in this book, how have my children done? Quite well actually.

"O" is up 116% in his two years of investing, for a compounded annual return of 45%.

"K" is up 129% in two years, for an annual return of 51%.

"A" is the winner so far. His portfolio is up 146% in the two year period, for a 57% compounded annual rate of return.

All three of them have done very well so far. Do I think it will continue? Probably not! The stock market on average returns roughly 10% per year, so what we have experienced these past few years (really, since the low point of the 2008 Financial Crisis) is an abnormal time. Stocks can't go up forever (or maybe they can!).

The point is not necessarily the great performance, but rather the process. By sticking to the blueprint, and using the pyramid, my children (like any new investor) are setting themselves up for a long and successful investing career.

CHAPTER 19-DON'T MAKE THE MISTAKES I'VE MADE

I've been investing and trading for nearly 30 years, and I've picked up a lot of good and bad habits along the way. Hopefully by now I have discarded most of the bad habits, but as far as mistakes go, boy I've made some big ones. You'll make the same mistakes too, unless you recognize the warning signs.

That said, here are five big mistakes I have made in my investing career. Reading my tales of woe will hopefully help you steer clear of my foibles!

Mistake #1-Averaging Down

More times than I care to remember a stock, future, option or forex currency pair I bought has dropped after I bought it. Sometimes I swear the market is out to get me, and it suckers me in at a high price, with an immediate drop once it knows I own it!

Conspiracy theories aside, many times after buying and witnessing a drop, I have thought "well, if I bought the stock at $10 a share, and thought it was a good deal at that price, I should buy even more at $8. After all, that will lower my average price, and now I am getting an even better deal on more stock!"

9 times out of 10, this was a bad idea, and I should not have listened to my inner voice.

When a stock goes down in price, it means something is wrong with the investment. For whatever reason, the market is telling you this is not a good stock. It may be temporary. You don't know. The point is clear-more people are selling this stock than buying. That is a warning sign.

The lure of averaging down is that your average entry price is lower, so your breakeven point after a few purchases has gone down. This sounds and feels pretty appealing until you realize this: you are throwing good money after bad!

One possible exception to this mistake is if you regularly invest. Say every month you put $100 in a mutual fund or ETF. In that case, sometimes you'll buy high, and sometimes you'll buy low. Over time, though you'll have a nice average price. Remember, even in this case, your pick eventually has to increase for you to benefit.

Some people get so enthralled with "bargain buying" that they actually enjoy buying on the way down. Trust me, though. Averaging down is not a good approach. Frequently you'll only end up with more of a bad investment.

Mistake #2-Treating Paper Profits As Play Money

Years ago, I remember my friends buying a local stock, Royal Appliance. This company made Dirt Devil vacuum cleaners, and many of us knew about the product and the company. Although I resisted, many friends invested when the company went public, and they were dancing a happy jig as the price soared. I forget the exact percentage, but I recall them bragging about their investment going up 5 or even 10 times their initial investment. Boy, did I feel dumb, and my regret in not buying was only amplified by their gloating.

Fast forward a few years, and all my friends still owned the stock. The bad news was that all those gains disappeared, and they were back to breakeven or worse.

"Paper profits, it wasn't real money," they rationalized.
WRONG ANSWER!

The money *was* real, and if they had sold before the stock crashed, they would have converted it to actual cash. Referring to it as paper profits-after the profits vanished-was a loser's way of rationalizing a bad investment decision (i.e., to not liquidate the stock before it collapsed).

The lesson here is NEVER view profits as "paper" profits. They are as real as cash profits, but just have not been converted to cash yet. Would you let someone steal your cash? Absolutely not! Then, don't let the market steal your unrealized gains. Protect your investment, for example, with a trailing stop exit. That way, if the stock tumbles, you get out before all your profit is gone.

Mistake #3-Refusing To Take A Loss

More times I care to admit, I bought a stock, obviously convinced of its future prospects. The market, though had other ideas. So, I watched my precious stock fall, many times in a sickening sort of death spiral. Occasionally it would recover, leaving me overjoyed. This is just the recovery's beginning, I mistakenly thought.

My hopes were soon dashed, and the stock kept dropping. But I usually held on-why? Was it ego, was it stubbornness, was it plain stupidity? Usually, it was all three. I was emotionally invested in my pick-after all, I was the genius who had picked it-and I could not admit I was wrong. That stock was a reflection of me and my abilities as a stock picker.

I'm sure I am not the only one to fall into this ego induced trap. And you'll never get very far if you refuse to admit you are wrong, and you refuse to take losses.

The simple fact is you will have bad picks. Just accept that. Great baseball players make outs 7 out of 10 times they bat. They are successful even with many failures.

The key with losing is to pick a price where you will throw in the towel-where you will admit you made a bad decision, and just move on. This is best done via a good till canceled stop loss order.

Before you even enter the position, know your exit point. If the stock is trading at $10, conceivably a drop to $7 is enough to convince you. Or $5. But, never $0!

You could base the exit on the stock price fall itself, but if the whole market is falling, maybe your stock is not as bad as you thought. So, understanding the reasons for the drop can help you decide whether to sell or not.

So, you can avoid this mistake by always having a stop loss active, placed at a price where you decide it is time to exit, lick your wounds, and move on to the next stock.

Refusing to take a loss is pretty much a sure way to sabotage your investing.

Mistake #4-Getting Out Too Early

As I mentioned in Mistake #3, too many times I held on to a losing stock longer than I should have. I've also made the opposite mistake for winning trades; getting out too early.

This is another psychological ego issue: the need to be right. Nothing feels better than picking a stock and immediately making money on it. I feel great, my spouse and kids are proud of me, and my friends and colleagues are all jealous. A perfect storm of genius!

Not wanting this euphoria to end, I decide to sell the stock at a profit. Cha-ching goes the cash register.

But months later, depression hits me. My genius stock pick kept going up, long after the applause from my victory subsided. What an idiot I am! I got out too early!!

This mistake is as awful as holding on to losers. True, it is foregone profits rather than losing hard cash that I am talking about, but the net effect is the same. Avoid this mistake and financially you'll be better.

The cure? Avoid exiting a rising stock, unless your view of it has changed, or if the market is telling you to exit. A trailing stop loss order is ideal here. It can ride below the stock price and slowly rise as the stock price rises (just don't let the trailing stop fall backwards–

always have it flat or rising). That way, you don't get out too early, you don't celebrate a pyrrhic victory, and you don't feed your ego with meaningless small profits.

One reason professional investors are professional is that they avoid making mistakes #3 and #4. They treat stock trading and investing like the business it is. Emotion does not influence successful investors.

Mistake #5–Trading Based On Other's Tips

Back when I first got into management in my former aerospace career, a manufacturing manager named Jay helped me along. He helped me avoid issues with the union workers, and he really helped me the first few months as a struggling engineer turned Quality Assurance manager. I am indebted to him for that.

So, as we became friends, and I listened to his advice, he'd feed me (and other coworkers) stocks tips once in a while. I remember the sparkle in his eyes as he told me about some hot internet stock called Asia Global Crossing (this was the late 1990s or early 2000s, if my memory serves me correctly). I forget exactly what it did-I think it involved undersea cables-but I figured if Jay was in, then it was a good idea.

Now a tip, by itself, is not bad. However, you have dig deeper. I should have asked Jay his entry, target and stop loss exit prices. In other words, what was his long-term plan?

Unfortunately, I was young and naïve, so I never asked Jay these questions. In fact, I never asked him any questions. I don't recall telling him I bought the stock based on his tip, and I'm equally sure I never told him I held on as it collapsed (It looks like I was guilty of mistake #3 also). I probably did not want to make him feel bad that this tip did not work out, as I valued both his friendship and his management counsel. Really, I was embarrassed for myself.

This taught me an important investing lesson, one I still follow today. First, I almost never listen to stock tips from friends, colleagues or relatives anymore. Second, if I do follow a tip, I ask a lot of questions, and I follow the tipper absolutely and precisely. If I think Jay has a good tip (he is a smart and experienced guy, after all), I'll mimic his actions 100%. I'll buy when he buys, I'll trail my stop loss like he does, and I'll exit when he does. All with no tears-if the stock loses, I am not mad at the tipster.   I might not use his future tips, but my decisions are all on me, not the tipster.

So, trading tips is not always a mistake. Just remember to exercise caution. Don't blame the source. Remember you always have the final decision.

By the way, wonder what happened to my friend Jay? We are Facebook friends these days, and he might not even recall this story if he reads this book. But he is enjoying a happy and well deserved retirement near a beach in Florida, probably spending some of his stock market winnings on cold beer, thick juicy steaks and family fun.

CHAPTER 20-RUNNING OFF
THE RAILS

You read about some mistakes I've made in the last chapter, so now that you know them, don't repeat them!

Most of this book, however, has focused on the good parts of stock investing-the upside. But investing in the stock market can go wrong, as the "graybeards" at my first job out of college experienced. Three areas where things can go haywire:

General Market Crash

If you invest for a long enough period, you will undoubtedly experience a market crash or prolonged downturn, where suddenly and swiftly (or slowly but surely) 10-50% of your account value may vanish. Needless to say, this can be very unsettling, especially if you are at a point in your life where you want to cash in and spend the money you've earned. So, my advice is just to expect a crash/downturn, and if Murphy's Law holds, expect it at the very worst possible time.

One thing you can do to reduce your risk is periodically cash in your stocks, well before you actually need them. Assume retirement is in 3 years. Maybe each year leading up to your retirement date you liquidate 25% of your portfolio. By retirement, you'll still have 25% left for possible future growth, and you will have gotten a good average selling price over the past 3 years.

Impatience

Stocks go up and down. It is easy to get frustrated with this, since it affects your portfolio performance. My kids experienced this firsthand during their 7 month adventure. Investor O jumped out to a very early lead, which really upset Investors A and K. Both of them wanted to sell their existing picks and buy different stocks in an attempt to catch up, just a month into it. Such impatience!

Eventually things evened out, without any portfolio changes. Remember, investing is a long term marathon. It is not a 100 yard dash. If you stick to the plan, and the plan is right, you will be rewarded. But, bumps will occur. Be mentally prepared for that.

Neglect

On one hand, you don't want to panic and sell a stock that has dipped a bit. You don't want to be watching every price change. Conversely, don't completely ignore performance either. Regardless of your holding period, you still should regularly review your stock's performance and make adjustments as required. Keep an eye on each stock, but don't over-watch.

CHAPTER 21-GAMESTOP AND THE RISE OF THE MILLENNIALS

One of the most interesting events that I have ever witnessed in the stock market unfolded in late 2020/early 2021. What was it, what lessons does it teach us and how can it help us in the future? That and more will be discussed in this chapter.

The Stock Market's Most Interesting Event Of The Century (So Far!)

In mid 2020, by all accounts GameStop (GME) was a dog of a stock. Its financials and fundamentals were poor, the executive suite was a revolving door and its future prospects were dim. The "glory days" for this company during the previous 2 decades seemed to be well behind it.

All this was apparent in the price of the stock:

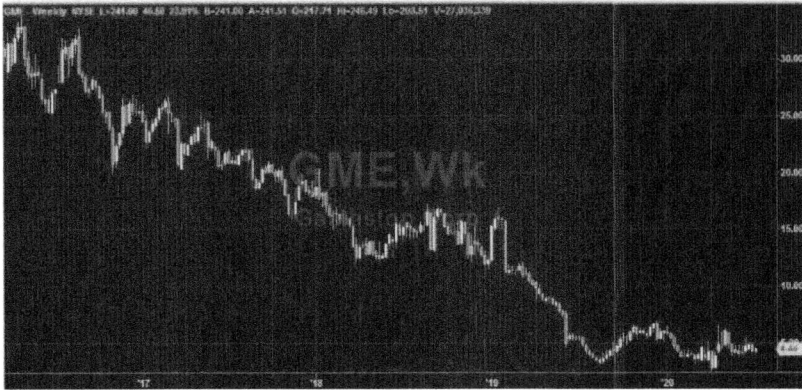

This was clearly a stock on its way down to zero. Wall Street hedge funds took notice of this, and started shorting the stock. For those unfamiliar, shorting the stock is a bet in anticipation of the stock price going lower. Normally, you buy low and sell high. Shorting just reverses the order; you sell high first, and later buy low.

Now, as you can imagine, Wall Street hedge funds are generally pretty smart, so if they were betting on a fall, then it was more than likely to actually happen.

All these factors added up made it fairly assured the stock was doomed. Except for one factor no one really accounted for: Millennials and the use of social media.

On the social media site Reddit.com, things started cooking amongst its members. Mad about Wall Street hoping for GameStop's demise and maybe partially lamenting the loss of a business they had grown up with (trading in old games and getting pennies on the dollar was no fun, but getting used games cheap was pretty cool), Millennials hatched a plan.

Now, I can't say it was a fully thought out coordinated effort, but the gist of it was: buy GameStop stock, and enough of us do, the price will rise and the hedge funds will be "short squeezed." A pretty audacious plan, to be sure.

However and whenever the plan was actually hatched, In September 2020 the price of GameStop started to rise, along with its daily volume:

They say nothing breeds success like success, and I believe that was the case here. The Millennials (and to be fair, probably many non-Millennials) started taking notice of the stock. People heard about the plan, and the short squeeze was on!

Over the next few months, the price absolutely skyrocketed:

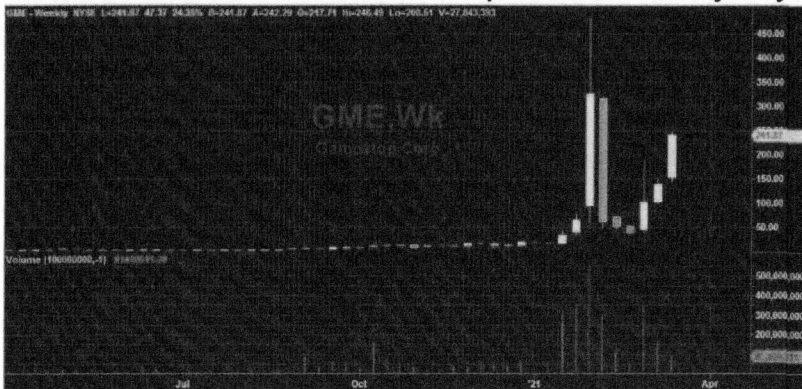

The hedge funds and others hoping for a price fall got absolutely crushed. Some hedge funds lost so much money they actually had to be bailed out by other hedge funds!

What happened in the annals of the stock market was unprecedented:

- A failing company's stock jumps 100 fold in the space of a few months, due primarily to social media manipulation. It also seesawed on a daily basis, sometimes by hundreds of dollars per share.

- • "Smart" Wall Street firms got steamrolled in the onslaught. Usually, those hedge funds are the steamroller!
- • GameStop became the most popular stock on the street for a time, with nearly limitless press coverage and social media posts.

Some of the early entrants to this event probably profited handsomely. Some of the latecomers, on the other hand, probably lost quite a bit.

Even though this was an unprecedented event, what lessons can we learn from it?

GameStop – Lessons Learned

Don't Try A Make A Quick Buck – once the drama unfolded, many people arrived too late, and bought GameStop thinking it was going to $1000. Of course, just as quickly as it rose, it fell – saddling many people with a big loss. Most people buying GameStop were simply gambling, and that is never a good idea.

Watch For Short Interest – you can easily get information on how much short interest is in a stock. Keep an eye on it, especially if you decide to go short! While many times shorts are smart money, they are subject to short squeezes. Stock shorting is not for beginners, and this debacle proves it.

Options Can Be Risky – many people bought options in GameStop instead of the actual stock. The problem is most people just don't understand options and how their price behaves relative to the underlying stock. That is not to say options aren't useful, but rather most beginner to intermediate traders should just stay away from them. The extra leverage they provide can be great, but that leverage cuts both ways; as your investment drops in value, leverage can really exacerbate the fall.

Have a Solid Plan BEFORE You Enter A Trade - Have a real plan before you trade, not some vague idea of what you want to do. As boxer Mike Tyson said: "Everyone has a plan until they get punched in the mouth." If you have a well thought out plan, when the stock punches you in the mouth, which it definitely did for many GameStop buyers, you'll be ready.

Watch Social Media And Stay Tuned In – Social Media is a force in the stock market. GameStop, along with some lesser stock and futures market plays in AMC and Silver, prove that point. Beware if you try to bet against the crowd. They may just run you over.

GameStop – How Can This Help You Going Forward?

While the whole experience with GameStop may be a once in a lifetime event, there will be other events that you can possibly take advantage of. The scenarios will be different, but there will always be unique occurrences in the market that make many of the "smart" people very rich.

So, my advice is to always keep your eyes and ears open for unique opportunities. When you see something before everyone else, jump in with appropriate position sizing!

CHAPTER 22-YOUR NEXT
STEPS AND WRAPPING UP

If you've made it this far, congratulations. Of course, now the real fun begins.

In the first few chapters, you learned enough about stocks, ETFs and investing to at least get started. The first step here is to acquire trading capital. Remember, treat this as money you can afford to lose. Don't mortgage your house just to start trading and investing.

With investment capital ready, open a brokerage account, after researching some major firms. Each has unique benefits, but many times a brokerage is a brokerage is a brokerage. If you pick one and dislike it, just transfer your funds to another one. The new brokerage will probably make it very easy, since each likes taking customers from the other.

Once you have the brokerage account open, determine where you want to be on the pyramid. I recommend starting at Tier 1. Just invest an amount in SPY or another benchmark ETF or mutual fund. Then, progress from there.

You may decide to next follow a newsletter, or instead follow a trading legend like Warren Buffett. Certainly you could do worse than following one of the greatest investors of all time.

As you climb the pyramid, the analysis and time commitment becomes more complicated and cumbersome. A lot of how far you climb will depend on your interests. I know plenty of folks who just invest at Tier 1 by buying a benchmark ETF and forget about it for a few decades. And I know others who create complicated trading algos to more accurately time and outperform the market.

Keep in mind that you can simultaneously invest in multiple tiers. For example, I have some retirement money at Tier 1, some market sector ETFs from Tier 3, stock picks from Tier 5, some algos running at Tier 7 (on stock indices in the futures market) and also some exotic investing via options and shorting in Tier 8. But, I can tell you I did not start at Tiers 7 and 8. The ideal journey starts at Tier 1.

While you are investing, remember to strive for diversification, and remember to review your performance regularly. The old wives tale "a watched pot never boils" applies here. Don't calculate your performance every day or every week. You'll drive yourself crazy stressing over the ups and downs. But, don't ignore the performance for more than 6 months. It is your hard earned money, so keep a close watch on it.

With that, I'll say goodbye, and wish you luck. I hope the future years bring you much investing success. Feel free to drop me a line and let me know how your investing is going.

Good Luck investing with the pyramid blueprint!

Printed in Great Britain
by Amazon

25907525R00071